Book 2: The Apparatus of the Law

LAW, CLASS AND SOCIETY

Book 2:

The Apparatus of the Law

by

D. N. PRITT

"Laws grind the poor, and rich men rule the law"
OLIVER GOLDSMITH

1971
LAWRENCE AND WISHART
LONDON

SBN: 85315 230 6

Printed in Great Britain
by The Camelot Press Ltd.,
London and Southampton

Contents

Contents

Introduction

IN the first volume of this series I dealt with the topic, very illuminating for students of politics and of life in general, of the law in its relations with employers and with workmen and their trade unions. In this second volume I treat of the law in its more general aspects and look at how it has grown and developed—and at how it has been used as a weapon of class struggle.

Law—the legislature, the judges and magistrates, the lawyers and the juries—is an important part of the machinery of government in every modern state. By "government" I mean not just administration but government in its widest sense, which controls, influences and shapes the whole way of life of a people, largely in the interest of the ruling class.

As Professor Pierre Cot, the distinguished French politician and jurist, wrote: "Le droit est la projection d'une civilisation" (roughly, the law of any country is the expression of its civilisation). In the first place, the law, in its general form and character, corresponds to the economic basis of a civilisation, that is to say, to the economic structure, forms of property and class structure. Thus, for example, a civilisation based on a feudal economy has a feudal system of law, and this feudal law becomes modified as feudal relations give place to capitalist ones, perhaps by comparatively gradual erosion and replacement, perhaps by revolutionary violence, into a system of capitalist law. In the second place, the whole of a civilisation— which is, of course, no abstract thing (any more than justice, or right, or truth can be abstract) but an immensely complex social organism—must be seen and understood as the product of all the forces at work in society. It is shaped and reshaped by the activities and strivings of the various classes.

The law is not, therefore, the merely automatic reflection

of a particular economic structure, but takes shape, develops and changes in ways determined by actual class interests and class struggles. As a result, law is determined above all by the work and the wishes of the dominant or ruling class—a body, great or small in membership, which largely determines a country's life, deciding upon its wars, making its peace treaties, imposing its taxes and, by the economic power conferred by ownership of property, managing the economy and so dictating how well or ill the main body of citizens shall live. This ruling class, one must bear in mind, changes with the passage of time, like everything else. It changes in its composition, its strength, the sources of its strength, its interests, and its problems; the degrees of opposition to it vary, and it changes accordingly its views as to how it should react, and whether it should appease, oppose, bamboozle, or destroy. (A ruling class may not only change, it may be displaced by a new one, at times gradually, as occurred in England with the passing of power from the landowners to the capitalists, and at times swiftly, by revolution.)

The ruling class by no means uses its power impartially for the benefit and protection equally of all classes that make up the community. Nor are its servants, including the legislators, judges and lawyers, in any sense neutral. It governs in its own interests, which it professes to believe, and perhaps sometimes does believe, to be identical with the interests of the whole people.

In most states, the ruling class is numerically a small minority of the population. This was indeed universally the position until the socialist revolution of 1917 in what was until then Tsarist Russia. The ruling class holds its power by virtue of its property in land, industry or finance, and enforces it by its command over armed forces and police. Yet for all this, its power is not unlimited or unchallengeable. In most countries, and certainly in Britain, it has always to take account of the wishes and resentments—and the actual or potential strength—of the majority of the people. The down-to-earth question: "Will they stand for that?" must have been asked in "the corridors of power" a thousand times; and public opinion has far greater strength than most people imagine, especially when it receives expression in organisation and demonstrative action. (We shall see this well illustrated, by contrast, when I come to deal in Book 3 with colonial problems, and describe how badly the various branches of colonial administration, including the law, have behaved in areas where the only effective public opinion is that of themselves, their colleagues in other branches, and a few professional and business men of similar views to themselves.)

Engels summed up the position as long ago as 27th October, 1890, in his well-known letter to Conrad Schmidt, as follows:

"In a modern state, law must not only correspond to the general economic condition and be its expression, but must also be an *internally coherent* expression which does not, owing to inner contradictions, reduce itself to nought. And in order to achieve this, the faithful reflection of economic conditions suffers increasingly. All the more so the more rarely it happens that a code of law is the blunt, unmitigated, unadulterated expression of the domination of a class—this in itself would offend the 'conception of right'. Even in the *Code Napoléon* the pure, consistent conception of right held by the revolutionary bourgeoisie of 1792–96 is already adulterated in many ways, and, in so far as it is embodied there, has daily to undergo all sorts of attenuations owing to the rising power of the proletariat. . . . Thus to a great extent the course of the 'development of right' consists only, first, in the attempt to do away with the contradictions arising from the direct translation of economic relations into legal principles, and to establish a harmonious system of law, and then in the repeated breaches made in this system by the influence and compulsion of further economic development, which involves it in further contradictions." (*Selected Works* of Marx and Engels, Lawrence and Wishart, London, 1968, page 697.)

Conflicts of this nature, involving a minority ruling class seeking to maintain and further its own interests against the majority, and giving way to resistance only as far as it must, can only cease when the majority becomes the ruling class. After that, we shall still have to cope with errors or misjudgments, but not with the selfish measures of a hostile and powerful minority. Meanwhile, in such countries as ours, the ruling class—if it is as intelligent as ours has nearly always proved to be—does not "drive too hard", but watches all the time to see how far it can go in serving its own interests without exciting too much opposition or even bringing about revolt or revolution; and the majority, actively or passively, by non-co-operation, boycotts, strikes, and many other forms of resistance short of revolt or revolution, gets something of its own way, delaying, hindering or modifying the plans of its rulers, and even compelling them to legislate in its own interests against their will (in a manner of which I have given a number of examples in Book 1: the most striking was the forcing through of the Trades Disputes Act, 1906, and the virtual dictation of its most important terms, described in Chapter 5 of Book 1).

It follows that the general body of the governed citizens are not wholly strangers to the formation and control of their machinery of government, including the law, and the citizen who says that he "has never had anything to do with the law" is in fact in contact with it all his days. It not merely declares his duties, and to some extent his rights, telling him what he may and what he may not do, and shaping, to a far greater degree than he realises or would admit, his thoughts and outlook, his "way of life", but he in his turn does a great deal to shape it. Consciously or unconsciously, he and his fellow-citizens contribute day by day to its formation and development, by their resistance to—or their acquiescence in—the proposals of their rulers, by their positive demand for reforms, and by their apparently intangible but real and indeed powerful influence in the formation of public opinion.

It follows that the working class today has much more influence on the development of our law than appears on the surface, and working people have a corresponding responsibility to maintain continuously the greatest possible pressure on public opinion and on the government to secure the most healthy development possible.

The whole body of our law should thus be regarded not as something wholly created and imposed on us from above by a ruling class, but rather as the work of many generations of English people, both of those who at the various stages of our history have had the direct power to shape it in their own interests, and of those who could do no more than obstruct or modify this shaping in varying degrees by their organised insistence or passive resistance.

Let me add, in conclusion, lest the picture of how our law is framed be presented as too simple and stark an affair of incessant class struggle, that by no means all the law—indeed, not all the legislation that is passed by modern parliaments—is designed to further class interests directly by imposing the will of the ruling class on the mass of the people. Much law, and some legislation, is "neutral" in the limited sense of being designed to govern the relations between individuals or groups in fields with no strong element of class conflict, where indeed the actual provisions of the law would be just as useful, and no more significant, if they were the opposite of what they are. For example, the law of England directs wheeled traffic to keep to the left; but there is no class interest directing traffic to keep to the left as there is directing politics to keep to the right. And the law of the sale of goods, which determines the precise moment at which the property in the goods passes to the buyer, does not form an essential part of the machinery of the class struggle, whereby the minority "keeps people in their places"; power and control would be no weaker or stronger if the law determined that property should pass earlier or later, although no doubt the rules were developed in accordance with the ruling-class view of what is best for the activities—in this instance, the commercial activities—of the community.

I

The Shape and Sources of Our Law

MANY people conceive of law in general, and of the law of
England* in particular, as consisting of precise statements in
Codes, pretty easy to understand and apply, and not readily
susceptible of being stretched or twisted to serve the ends of a
government, a ruling class, or a rich litigant, so that the volume
of cases which have to be fought out in the Courts between the
state and citizens, or between citizen and citizen, should be
small, and should consist mostly of disputes of fact, and not
turn on doubts as to what the law provides, or on questions as
to whether a particular set of facts, once proved, does or does
not give a right to some legal remedy.

Such a conception can seldom be accurate in relation to any
country, and certainly not any capitalist country, if only because the contests to which the law may have to be applied in
concrete cases, and the questions of fact which have to be
decided in nearly every case before the law can be applied, are
of such variety and complexity that there can seldom be much
certainty as to the result that should rightly be reached when
the facts and the law have been ascertained. Many cases will
turn mainly on questions of fact—often very difficult questions—
and many elements of human bias or prejudice or mere common
sense will contribute to their determination, and this determination may be accurate or inaccurate—may indeed be challenged
and altered by courts of appeal established by reason of all the
uncertainties involved. And, equally, when the law comes to be
stated and applied to these facts, elements of human bias or
prejudice or of mere common sense—with, inevitably if unconsciously, the class outlook of those who have to state the
law—will contribute to the formulation of the statement; and

---

* As I explained in Book 1, I write of "England" here, and not of Britain, because
English and Scots law are very different from one another.

the law may be, or may appear to the litigants, and to others, to be stretched or twisted in the process.

Thus, law precisely stated and easily understood and applied is probably impossible of achievement, even in states which have brief and well-drawn Codes such as the *Code Napoléon* and its many derivatives; certainly, anything of the sort is impossible in England, whose law is, for historical reasons, especially shapeless and difficult to state briefly or comprehensively.

Let me start by explaining its sources. There is the "Common Law", which I will discuss in detail in Chapter 2; Equity, which comes in Chapter 3; Legislation, in Chapter 4; Case Law —"Judicial Legislation", in Chapter 5; and the Constitution, in Chapter 6.

2

The Common Law

THE main and primary source of English Law is the "Common Law". It is a body of civil and criminal law which has grown up gradually, and has been developed—in a sense largely created—by "case law", sometimes called "judicial legislation". It consists of judgments of the courts, stating the law applying to the particular cases that come before them—and operating not merely as decisions of these cases but also as precedents of law applicable in subsequent cases—and thus gradually building up a body of law. This process has now gone on for so long that there are over 300,000 reported decisions which lawyers have to study in order to ascertain what the law is, and to unearth and cite some of them (as what is called "authority") in the cases they have to conduct. I shall have to discuss "judicial legislation" at greater length in Chapter 5; for the moment I mention it only in relation to its function as at once a source and a repository of the common law.

Our common law owes nothing to Roman law, which forms the basis of the laws of many European and Latin-American countries, and (by a historical exception) of one only of the fifty States forming the U.S.A., namely Louisiana. The rest have what is generally called "Anglo-Saxon" law, a term used to describe the law of those countries which follow English law. The founders of most of the North American states, and of the U.S.A. itself, took the English conceptions of law with them when they emigrated from England to America.*

England has drawn only to a modest extent and in certain special fields on the Roman law—for example in the law relating to probate of wills—which were never covered by the

* Louisiana was bought from France by the U.S.A., and retained its own French law. It is curious that, in general, colonising or conquering states leave their victims that much of their "way of life"; Tsarist Russia allowed the parts of Poland which it ruled for so long to retain their Roman law, and the English treated Quebec, captured from the French, in the same way.

common law, and do not call for separate study in this work. The common law was a purely native growth; it was called "common" because it was gradually accepted as applying commonly throughout the country, as distinct from other rules or customs which were confined to certain counties.

One set of rules of foreign origin did become part of the common law, namely the "law merchant" (simply, commercial law). It dealt mainly with international trade, and its rules were pretty generally accepted by all the European trading nations in the Middle Ages. They were very different from those of the common law, especially in relation to Bills of Exchange, where they gave the law of contract a flexibility which must have horrified orthodox native English lawyers. As trade developed between England and the Continent it was found helpful—indeed, probably, essential—for the smooth operation of valuable trade to apply these flexible rules, and not the rigid native English law, which was as different from that of the Continent as our weights and measures are to this day. The "law merchant" was absorbed gradually into the common law, of which it has long formed an integral part. It is an interesting example of "judicial legislation" that this absorption was carried through simply by the judges applying it to cases, and not by Parliament. (From time to time, Acts of Parliament have been passed to amend the law merchant, just as they have been to amend other parts of the law. They are often called "Mercantile Law Amendment Acts".)

The common law was, and apart from a quantity of piece-meal codification still is, "unwritten law". This does not mean that its provisions have never been written down in one form or another, but that it has never been officially and authoritatively expressed in a Code. To ascertain it for the purposes of application to any particular case, one has to search the precedents I have mentioned. Often, of course, the law governing a case will be known to the judges and lawyers engaged in it, and no citation of "authority" will be needed unless and until the precise limits of some piece of the law proves to be necessary to the determination of the case. Often, too, the seeker for any applicable provision of the common law will find it conveniently —but in no sense authoritatively—stated in text-books, of which there are perhaps too many, of varying merit.

I mentioned piecemeal codification above. The position is that, whilst there is still no Code of the common law, a good many sections of it, including a good deal of the "law merchant" and most of the criminal law, have been codified in various Acts of Parliament in the last hundred years.* Even then the ingrained habit of English lawyers of "going to the precedents" to find the law has persisted so strongly that the judges have often had to remind them that, when a section of the law has been codified, the law to be applied is to be found in the provisions of the statute and not in the cases enshrining the old unwritten law which lay at the root of the codifying statute.

---

* In British India, where over wide fields the law of England, with or without modifications, had to be applied by judges, magistrates, advocates, and civil servants, many of whom had not complete command of the English language, and to some of whom English legal conceptions and procedures were strange, it was found pretty early that it was essential to codify most of the English common law to make it possible for them to understand and apply it. The work, fortunately, was done extremely well; and on one occasion, when I was arguing a case before the Supreme Court of India some years after independence, I remarked *en passant* that the British had at least conferred that benefit on India, whilst not giving its people at home the same advantage. I was rewarded by warm smiles from the very erudite lawyers who formed the Court; they plainly agreed with me.

3

Equity

FOR some centuries, the common law which I described in the previous Chapter was substantially all the law, civil and criminal, that prevailed in England. I have now to relate the curious history of an important additional field and source of law, called "Equity", which today, side by side with the common law, governs the activities of a society far and away more elaborate than that which was originally covered by the common law in a country of two or three million people living rather poorly and simply on an island lying on the outer edge of the then civilised world.

Equity, nowadays often called Chancery because it was and is in the domain of the Lord Chancellor, took some time to become an integral part of our law. It is now so much an integral part of it that many lawyers, if asked whether a particular point with which they were dealing was derived from the common law or from equity, would have to think for a while before they could answer.

Equity came into being because the common law, which was meant to cover, and in simpler days had covered, all the activities of society, was—like most early legal systems—pretty rigid, and gradually became manifestly incomplete in that it contained no provisions covering many activities which a developing society had brought into being. The "causes of action"—as lawyers label any right to have some relief from the court—which it recognised were expressed in and covered by a limited number of "writs", and if any citizen's grievance, which might be both legitimate and important, was not covered by a known "writ", the courts could give him no remedy. As society grew, and more and more new matters and problems arose, calling urgently for new remedies, the courts—driven no doubt by the feeling that they ought to provide machinery

to cover the whole of man's activities, expressed in the Latin
tag: *Boni judicis est ampliare jurisdictionem* ("It is the function of
a good judge to extend his jurisdiction")—attempted to fill the
gap by enlarging the application of some of the existing writs.
Their efforts did not succeed, and some other solution had to be
found. This took a curious but in the end highly successful
form. Citizens began to petition the King to remedy grievances
not covered by the common law, and the King referred the
petitions to his principal minister, the Lord Chancellor. The
latter, who was often a lawyer, at first dealt with the petitions
broadly, deciding as he thought "just and equitable". Then
from this, as the petitions grew in volume, there slowly grew
up a body of law—inevitably, of case law—applied in trials
before the Lord Chancellor or his deputies, sitting in courts
established to administer "equity". This body of law, built
up by these decisions, had hardened, long before the nineteenth
century arrived, into law in the fullest sense, well-established
and substantially as rigid as the common law itself. The name
"Equity" remained, but the conception of equity as something
"equitable" and more flexible and "free and easy" than a
fixed system of law had faded away. The courts of equity or
Chancery, although perhaps a little more generous than the
common law courts in the interpretation of their law, could
not and did not any longer decide cases merely on a view of
what they might think just and equitable, without regard to the
already established precedents of their system of equity.*
There were thus—and indeed still are—two bodies of law in
England, common law and equity, existing side by side. They
were applied by two separate and independent sets of courts
until 1875, when all the courts (including those which
applied some Roman Law) were fused into one "Supreme Court
of Judicature", empowered to apply both common law and
equity. Since then, law and equity, and the small fields where
Roman Law comes into play, together constitute a complete
system of law which can rightly be called the Law of England.
Some matters—Roman Law apart—are, as they were before,
covered by the common law and some by equity (in some
matters, before 1875, it had even been necessary for the two

* There is a curious half-parallel to this system of creating new law and new
courts in the development of appeals from the colonies to the Judicial Committee
of the Privy Council, with which I shall deal in Chapter 7.

sets of courts to co-operate to provide satisfactorily both a cause of action and an adequate remedy!). Now, as I have said, one court can deal with all the causes of action, and give the necessary remedies.

Where there is a real or apparent conflict between the two systems, the common law giving rights to one person whilst equity gives them to another, "equity prevails". For example, one man may have the legal title, ownership, recognised by the common law in a piece of land, whilst equity holds that the beneficial or "equitable" title rests in another person. In such a case, which arises most commonly under the law of trusts, where the trustee holds the common law title but is bound in equity to give the whole advantage and use of the property to the beneficiary, the "prevalence" of equity would in the last resort be secured by the effective method of sending the trustee to prison for contempt of court so long as he continued to disobey the order to give the benefit of the property to the beneficiary.

While the courts were thus fused, the two separate laws were left separate and intact. They still exist separately, for judges and lawyers to understand and apply.

4

Legislation

THE next main source of law is called "statute law", i.e. laws created by Acts of Parliament, which are commonly called statutes; these are used both to amend existing law and to create new law. The legislative power of Parliament is un-limited. For example, in both the World Wars Parliament passed statutes to prolong its own existence beyond the statutory limit (seven years at the period of the First and five years at that of the Second), for one statute of the omnipotent legislature could override another.

There are about 3,000 Acts of Parliament wholly or partly in force, some of them running back seven centuries, and new statutes are passed at the rate of one hundred or more each year. The older statutes are short and simple; the modern ones long, complicated, and difficult to understand. They are drawn with every intention that they should be certain—not that they should be comprehensible on a first reading but that, in the end, after prolonged study by lawyers, they should have definite meanings, with not too much doubt as to what those meanings are! Even so, it is notorious among lawyers that questions of interpretation are the most uncertain of all questions of law coming before the courts, and that one court will disagree with another—even angrily—over such questions. I had a case some years ago in the House of Lords, in which the question of the exact meaning of a clause made a difference of a small fraction of a penny per 100 gallons of water supplied by one water authority to another, and thus to many thousands of pounds a year. My clients succeeded at first instance; the other side carried the case to the Court of Appeal, where their arguments prevailed; and my clients, confident that they were right, went on to the House of Lords. There, all the five judges conceived of an interpretation which had never occurred to either of the parties, and it proved impossible to move them. We left the court thinking that we should have been better off if we had never litigated at all, for the House of Lords invention— for that was what it seemed to be—looked disastrous for my clients, financially, in the long run. (But when I met them some years later, they told me that it had actually worked out heavily in their favour!)

What is called "delegated legislation", or "subordinate legislation", is sometimes treated as a separate source of law, but it is not really so. It consists of a vast volume of "statutory instruments" (formerly called "statutory rules and orders") drafted and issued by government departments, and having the force of law because various statutes have expressly empowered the departments to make them. The departments have no power to legislate beyond what is thus given to them, and the validity of their "enactments" can be tested in the courts as being "ultra vires", i.e., beyond the powers given to the department, if it can be shown that the legislation or some part of it does not fall within the powers given by the Act of Parliament.

In form, this delegated legislation normally consists of "Orders in Council", made in theory by the Privy Council, a body formerly of the greatest importance, whose functions— apart from such special activities as those of the Judicial Committee noticed above, with which I shall deal further in Chapter 7—now consist mainly in the formal expression of decisions taken by government departments. An Order in Council bringing in delegated legislation will state in its preamble the powers given by Parliament to enact it,* and in most cases the Orders can be disallowed by Parliament by Resolution, without the need to pass an Act of Parliament to annul them.

Since delegated legislation is prepared by civil servants— legally qualified, of course—and does not go through any process of scrutiny or amendment as Bills do in Parliament (of which lawyers sometimes complain that the final version is more incomprehensible than the original), it is in fact often poorly drafted and leads to trouble when interpreted and applied by the courts. Practising lawyers, rightly or wrongly, maintain

---

* At times Orders in Council are made wholly or partly in the exercise of "the prerogative", that is, of powers not derived from statute but still retained by "the Crown", as the government is called in such contexts. They are the remnants of the great power exercised by the King in past centuries.

that no one can be a good draftsman if he merely sits in an office, and does not undergo the severe discipline of arguing things out in court or by other controversial discussion.*

I shall write further about the difficulties of interpretation in Chapter 11.

* I recall a case in which the two contestants, arguing as to the true meaning of a piece of "delegated legislation", were of one mind that there were two and only two possible interpretations of the clause involved, so that we could expect the court to accept one or other of them, and the court did so. I was content, for my clients' view, which seemed sensible, had prevailed, and I thought that they were what the departmental draftsman had intended. But some time later I chanced to meet a high official of the department, and he told me that he was the draftsman of the clause. I asked him which of the two meanings he had intended, and was surprised when he answered: "My dear fellow, you practising lawyers do not understand simple English. I did not intend anything that either of you was talking about. To me it is quite plain, and presents no difficulty. I will tell you what it means." And he went on to give a meaning which no judge or practising lawyer could or would have attached to the words he had used.

5

Case Law—"Judicial Legislation"

FINALLY I come to discuss the complicated and emphatically "Anglo-Saxon" source of law, called case law, and occasionally "Judicial Legislation". This very elaborate system of developing the law, applying equally to common law and equity, indeed to the entire field of law, is based on the practice of the courts holding themselves bound to follow previous decisions of the courts on matters of law. It is unknown, in its full form, outside the "Anglo-Saxon" legal systems. Lawyers in all countries, of course, attach a good deal of importance to previous decisions of the courts of their own countries, and to some extent to those of others whose legal systems are similar, but in all the "non-Anglo-Saxon" countries, precedents—decisions in previous cases, or rather the reasoning underlying them—are no more than a part of the material which courts use in arriving at their decisions. The courts do not treat them as binding, and they are free to reject the reasoning if they do not agree with it. But in England the position is very different, and more rigid. Precedents are binding, and there is something like an etiquette, or a book of rules, telling the courts what they may or may not do in the way of departing from earlier decisions. Every court of first instance must treat the judgments of appellate courts as binding on it—as it is called, as "authority"—in the sense that it must accept as correct the law laid down in them, and apply it to the cases before it, whether it believes it to be correct law or not. (This restriction on the courts' freedom of judgment is labelled with the Latin tag *stare decisis*—"abide by what has been decided".) Courts remain at liberty, of course, to find grounds, if they can, for holding that there are differences on the facts of a case which render the reasoning of the earlier decisions inapplicable. This is called "distinguishing" the authority.

To return to the "etiquette", a court of first instance is not bound to follow previous decisions of a court of equal rank to itself, although it will naturally pay great respect to any such decision and agree with it if it feels that it can. When one comes to the next step upwards, one finds that an appellate court must follow decisions of courts of equal rank (which means that the Court of Appeal must follow its own decisions, as well of course as those of the House of Lords, and that the House of Lords must normally follow its own decisions too). Quite recently, however, the House of Lords has declared that it no longer regards itself as actually bound to do so, and early in 1969 one judge in the Court of Appeal, dissenting from his colleagues, declared that the Court of Appeal ought to give itself the same freedom as the House of Lords.

It may well be that in the near future, since the "book of rules" has no legal sanction and the courts are free to determine their own rules, the Court of Appeal may change its mind. Rapidly as change comes about nowadays, even in the law, I feel that it will be a long time, however, before the courts have the same freedom to follow or to reject precedent as non-Anglo-Saxon courts have, for the obligatory case law system is deeply embedded in our whole law and practice. The recent "freedom" declared by the House of Lords is primarily due to the realisation that there are every now and then decisions even of that very efficient tribunal which are seen afterwards by the profession to be clearly wrong. But, whatever be the reasons for the change of practice, we must in future bear in mind, when considering the possibilities of attacks by the courts on the trade unions—with which I dealt particularly in Chapters 5, 11, and 12 of Book 1—that House of Lords decisions which we have for better or worse regarded as immutable, may hereafter be altered to the advantage of one side in the struggle or the other.

The Privy Council, the ultimate Court of Appeal from Dominions and Colonies, which is regarded as of equal rank with the House of Lords, has always held itself free not to follow its own previous decisions, but in practice it is extremely difficult to persuade it not to do so!

Our case law system grew up gradually as part of the development of our law. In early days, there were naturally few precedents, and the judges had to work out as best they could what was, or rather what should be, the law governing some new set of facts, on the basis of such principles as our rather shapeless law provided, and with an infusion of common sense and their own conceptions of what was just and reasonable—conceptions based, of course, on the outlook they derived from their education and circumstances. As time went on, and precedents accumulated, the whole field of human activity became pretty well covered by cases already decided, in the sense that authority could be found near enough to every case that arose to give the court a guide to its decision. This did not mean, of course, that the process of building up the law by case law was at an end, but merely that there was no unoccupied territory. There still remained two activities for the courts and the lawyers. The first and most important lay in adapting the law to new social ideas and developments of human activity. This has been so neatly done through the centuries—within the limits and according to the lights of the ingrained outlooks of the lawyers—by the application of the principles of law which case law had gradually established, that the law, which started with a small nation mainly engaged in agriculture, and with the employment of one man by another in workshops or on the land on a small and rather personal basis, has grown, without any violent upheaval, into an elaborate system serving efficiently a vast capitalist and industrial country. The second activity was and is that of using the ingenuity of lawyers to make endless refinements in case law to further the interests of the ruling class and of private—and often very rich—clients.

One can indeed think of the history of case law as passing through two rather different stages. In the first, the courts were consciously or unconsciously building a system of law out of nothing or very little; and in the second, they have more and more been refining and sharpening an already existing system of law by a stream of new decisions, interpreting and applying it to case after case, and in the process fighting in fact, whether they wholly realised it or not, the class struggle. It is naturally in this second phase that case law interests us for the purposes of this book, and that the question whether case law is really legislation comes to the front.

I turn now to consider the merits and defects of case law as it operates today, and to see how far it is correct to say that the judges do in reality legislate.

Let me start with the merits. The first is its flexibility. It is undoubtedly clear that a country with a well-developed case law system and efficient judges can keep its law flexible and up-to-date by the steady application of "authority" to new situations and circumstances, so that, at times when social and economic developments are moving relatively slowly, there is little or no need for Acts of Parliament to change or add to the law. For centuries, the volume of our legislation was very small indeed, and it has only been in the nineteenth and twentieth centuries that it has been found necessary to pass hundreds of often very long Acts of Parliament to cope with economic and political developments.

The flexibility of case law was in the early centuries a real merit. Case law built up the whole of the common law, which—looked at from a detached and lawyerly point of view, and without regard to the function of law as a weapon of the ruling class—was and is a pretty good and workable system, if intolerably expensive in operation. And even today, in practice, important and sometimes genuinely beneficial developments of law are brought about by decisions.

Seeking in my rather varied experience for a fine example of this good working, I find the most striking one in the work done by the Privy Council in deciding a long string of cases on the Constitution of Canada. It is perhaps a pity that I have to go to the law of another country, in another Continent, for my example of how English judges do their work, but I find it such a good one that I would like to stand by it. The Constitution of Canada was the earliest of a number of constitutions of large federations of colonies. It was brought into being by the British North America Act, 1867, a piece of legislation which expressed, in some parts rather clumsily, agreements arrived at with great difficulty by long negotiation between representatives of many conflicting interests, religious, racial, economic, and others, in the colonies which were being amalgamated into one Dominion. It was a great political achievement, but it was also a fertile field of doubt, confusion, and litigation, many of its provisions being difficult to interpret.* When from time to time the people

* I was once engaged in a case arising out of the difficult provisions of this Constitution, relating to education, where the conflicting interests of Catholics and Protestants had not made agreement easy. The city of Montreal had at first a large Catholic and a large Protestant population, the latter consisting largely of

of Canada wished to amend their Constitution they found that the only legal method of doing so, since it was an Act of the Parliament at Westminster, lay in that Parliament, which included of course no Canadian representatives, passing another Act! There was a good deal of resentment, which was ultimately cured by legislation, with which we need not concern ourselves here. What is pertinent for us is the way in which the Privy Council dealt with the problems which frequently arose as to the meaning of many of the provisions of the Constitution. These problems came before the courts of the Canadian Provinces, and before the Supreme Court of Canada, in litigation either between private citizens or between the Provinces and the Dominion; and many of these decisions were carried up to the Privy Council on appeal. The total volume of these decisions, in each of which the Privy Council followed its own previous decisions, gradually built the Constitution up into an intelligible and consistent law, which the original negotiators might scarcely have recognised. All this work attracted little attention in England, for it did not directly concern us, but it provides the fullest and strongest illustration— known to me because I was engaged in a good many of the cases—of how flexible and adaptable and constructive judicial legislation can be, within its class structure. It also provides much of the affirmative answer to the question: can case law amount to legislation? to which I shall have to return.

Let me now turn to some of the defects of the case law system as we apply it in England. I make two main points against it. The first is that its virtue of flexibility may prove to be a defect, inasmuch as the development of law by this method may work against the true interest of the majority of the population, and the second is that in actual operation the elucidation and development of the law by case law is slow, expensive and haphazard.

"Black" protestants from Northern Ireland. The agreed provisions worked relatively well for some years, but after a time a large influx of Jews into the city created problems, which were solved, again for a time, by the theologically inadequate legislative provision that, in the city, for the purposes of education, Jews should be deemed to be Protestants. This broke down in its turn, not because Jews objected to being called Protestants, but because the Protestants were alarmed by the increase of the proportion of Jews in the population, which led to a serious risk that the governing body, called "the Protestant Board of School Commissioners", would shortly have a majority of Jews in its membership.

On the first of these points, the governing feature is one of which I wrote a good deal in Chapter 5 of Book 1, when dealing with the famous decisions of the House of Lords in the "Taff Vale" and "Osborne" cases. I emphasised there how strongly men's surroundings affect their outlook, and pointed out that almost all the judges are drawn from surroundings very different from those of most of the people over whom they exercise jurisdiction. The practical result, in relation to what we are considering here, is that when judges come to decide new points, and to apply thereto principles of law already established, they inevitably approach them from their own point of view, which they derive from their education, upbringing and outlook, of what is socially good or bad. It may— indeed, it almost must—follow that each step in the development of the law taken by court decisions is, to a greater or lesser degree, a step in the direction of consolidating the point of view, and serving the interests, of the ruling class. Thus, case law has for some centuries been tending to favour one side of the class war, be it the landlord, the employer, the industrialist, or more generally, the apparatus of government, against the "man in the street". Thus does the apparent merit of case law turn out to be a defect, and the observation of the establishment poet, Tennyson, that:

> "Freedom slowly broadens down
> from precedent to precedent"

should really be amended by replacing the word "broadens" by "narrows".

I shall return to this topic in Chapter 7.

On the second point, that case law in its development works badly, there are a number of considerations. To begin with, as I mentioned on p. 49 of Book 1, it is of the nature of case law that no precedent can be created until some concrete case, raising the particular problem, not only arises but involves a litigant who is both willing and able to spend money fighting the case, with the knowledge that after he has incurred all the expense of the trial at first instance, the matter will very likely be carried to appeal—indeed, to two successive appeals— but because it does involve an important and undecided point of law. It is a matter of pure chance how long one may have to wait before such a case, equipped with such a willing litigant, may arise, whereas the normal method of clearing up or improving the law, legislation, can be undertaken by Parliament—no doubt, with some small delay—whenever the real need for it is manifest. One point of law, which arose because legislation in the eighteenth century laid down that contracts of insurance, which are, when one analyses them, of the nature of wagers—since they involve the payment of money by one person to another on the happening of an event which is not certain to happen—and wagering contracts in general are unenforceable in the courts, should be fully valid if and only if the insurer has what is called an "insurable interest" in the subject matter of the risk involved, i.e., a genuine financial or economic or other legitimate interest, and not a mere gambler's hope of gain. This gave rise to a question whether a man had an insurable interest in his wife's life, and that question (which better drafted legislation might have settled from the start) created doubts and difficulties for many moneyed families. It was typically a problem for the courts to settle when a case arose in which they could do so. A case did so arise; and the courts did decide that a man has such an interest; but it took 168 years of waiting before the case arose! I myself conducted a case some years ago in the House of Lords under the Workmen's Compensation Acts, where an in truth absurd decision of the Court of Appeal, which had deprived a whole generation of workmen of compensation to which they were plainly entitled, was got rid of. The chanciness of the whole thing was illustrated in that case by the fact that the particular man who brought the case was unwise enough not to belong to a trade union which could have fought the case for him, and thus was able to sue only because his solicitor agreed to act for him without a fee, and asked me to do the same thing (which I did in order to get rid of a bad precedent for the benefit of all workmen).

So much for the point that case law legislation is slow, capricious and haphazard. That it is expensive is just part of the general high cost of litigation in England, increased by the fact that a really important test case on a doubtful point is almost certain to go to appeal. But what makes litigation expensive here? One element is that our shapeless law depends on an unwieldy mass of precedents, and is bedevilled by the fact that in any but the simplest case involving a question of law its great uncertainty makes it difficult for even the best and most conscientious lawyer to tell his clients with any confidence whether they will win or lose their case, so that many more cases are tried out than would be the case if there were more certainty.*

Another defect is that, coupled with this uncertainty, litigation in general, and in particular the various minor contests over procedural points that crop up in nearly every case, give the litigant who has the longer purse—and some of them have very long purses—great opportunities not just to "last the course" but to make the running intolerably costly for his poorer opponent by embarking on all sorts of these minor contests, called "interlocutory" proceedings, not necessarily unreasonable in themselves but involving a devastating burden of expense which I will discuss further in Chapter 11. The poorer litigant is often driven by financial necessity to "settle" (i.e., to compromise) a case on unfavourable terms, or even never to launch it at all, because he knows that he cannot face the cost of fighting a rich opponent at first instance, with the often grave risk of the case being carried to appeal. Thus, we have the serious injustice that many cases are "decided" not on lines which appear just to a court but by the weaker party never starting at all.

This is, of course, part of a wider injustice, inevitable in an unequal society, and fully curable only by fundamental social changes, but it looks extremely acute when one is examining litigation. I had an extreme example of the "long purse" in a case which I conducted in three courts a good many years ago. By pure chance the long purse was there confronted by long obstinacy on the part of my clients. The plaintiffs were an immensely powerful company, with assets worth hundreds of

---

* I can illustrate the practical difficulties of applying the vast mass of precedents in our case law by relating a case of mine where neither myself nor my opponent had been able to find, after long research, any very direct authority—that was usual enough, even for those who had as good a memory for the case law as I had—and the judge, drawing on his memory, said he was sure that there was a quite direct precedent if only we would seek further—that again is usual enough. I did not believe that we could all have missed the precedent, but as was our duty we went on searching, and at the very end of the arguments my opponent came into court and said that he had found what the judge had in his memory. He produced the report and there it was, right in the point and in my favour. That was just as well for my reputation, for the report showed that I had myself conducted the case!

millions, who had openly boasted that, whenever they litigated, they fought the other side to a standstill by running up the costs, and drove it to settle on terms favourable to the long purse. They were able to boast, too, that they had by these means never lost a case. The defendants, two individuals, were not poor. They disposed not of millions but of £50,000. When they were sued, they came to me and said that they were as stubborn as the plaintiffs, whom they hated, that they thought £50,000 was enough to see the case through even on the scale of expenditure which the plaintiffs were sure to adopt, and that they would rather go bankrupt than give in. So we fought. It was a difficult case, but I felt pretty strongly that we could win it.

The first thing the plaintiffs did was to suggest that the parties should share the cost of producing transcripts of the shorthand notes of the hearing, to be prepared and delivered first thing the following morning. This is quite usual in long cases, and much of the cost of it is eliminated by the fact that it helps the proceedings along so well that the resulting saving of time may well save the costs of one or two days; but—and here came the long purse—they also suggested that the notes should be printed instead of simply typed. This was unusual, and very expensive, and the proposal was, so to speak, the first declaration of an expense war. My clients thought that it would be bad tactics to seem anxious about money, so they agreed. Round one to us, but costly. The next move by the plaintiffs was more sinister. They were employing two K.C.s as well as a junior, and their leading K.C. was one of the best and most expensive available. He began to open the case to the judge and a jury. It was a long case, and it took him a few days. In the middle of his opening speech he made an application to the judge for leave to make serious amendments to the pleadings (i.e., as I shall explain in Chapter 11, the documents which stated the cases of the parties and thus defined the issues) designed to accuse my clients of seven or eight serious acts of dishonesty, thus widening the whole case, and of course greatly increasing the length of the trial and the consequent expense. The attitude of my stubborn and confident clients was that the charges were all nonsense, that they could refute them completely, and that—expense apart—the new move helped us by showing how reckless and irresponsible the plaintiffs were. My attitude, expressed in open court, was that, once such charges were even suggested in open court in the presence of the jury, no litigant with any respect for his reputation, and that included my clients at any rate, could resist the granting of leave so that the charges could be publicly refuted; and we therefore consented to the amendment. The case had to be adjourned for the pleadings to be put in order and for further preparation of evidence. When it came on again a few weeks later there were no major "new tricks", and the case was fought out, with some bitterness.

The jury returned a verdict against my clients on the original charge, and in their favour on all the added charges, and the judge gave judgment against my clients on that basis, for a substantial sum. My clients asked me what I thought of their prospects on appeal. I replied that in my view, as a matter of law, the plaintiffs had no cause of action on the original charge, and as they had already lost on all the others, an appeal offered good prospects. My clients said that I need not add the usual words of caution about the dangers of litigation, as they felt more stubborn than ever, and off we went to the Court of Appeal. All courts have "days off", on which they behave foolishly, and this court not merely dismissed our appeal but laid down the law in terms which would have made nonsense of an important piece of contract law if it had been allowed to stand. My clients asked me: "Are you still sure you are right?", to which I said that I was, and off they went to the House of Lords. There, after quite a struggle, we won, straightened up the law, and gave the heroes of the long purse and its invulnerability a heavy blow. The £50,000 with which my clients had started was gone, and a good bit more too, but we of course got an order for the costs in all three courts. My clients were not greatly out of pocket, and the plaintiffs lost their "invulnerability". I do not actually know of any other case where the determined use of the long purse was defeated by the stubbornness of the poorer men.

I have still to discuss the question whether "judicial legislation", i.e., the gradual operation of one decision after another in case law, or even occasionally a single decision, can truly be ranked as a form of legislation, a "source of law", bringing into the law some rule or provision which did not previously

c

exist (with, incidentally, the undemocratic and politically irresponsible result that legislation is carried through piece-meal, without programme or system, by non-elected persons holding posts to which they were not appointed on the basis of their legislative capacity or experience, and legislating only when, so to speak, some litigant rings a bell to give them the opportunity to legislate on one particular point). I think that, prior to the decision of the House of Lords in the case of Shaw v. Director of Public Prosecutions, reported in the Law Reports, [1962] A.C. 226, lawyers would have said that the answer to this question would be a matter of degree, in the sense that if one looked at any ruling of a court that seemed to carry the law quite a bit further than it had travelled before, some critics would say: "This is no more than a proper and legitimate development of good old-fashioned case law", whilst others would say: "This really amounts to legislation. The judge ought not to have gone so far, but should have said, as judges have often said, to counsel arguing for the decision he has in fact made: 'I wish that that were the law, but it is not. You are really asking me to make law, and that I cannot do. I can only interpret the law. To get what you are asking for, you must go to Parliament' ". The ruling generally cited on that point is that of Lord Esher, the Master of the Rolls, in the Court of Appeal, in Willes v. Baddeley, reported in the Law Reports, [1892] 2 Q.B., 324:

> "There is in fact no such thing as judge-made law, for the judges do not make the law, though they frequently have to apply existing law to circumstances as to which it has not previously been authoritatively laid down that such law is applicable."

It is still, no doubt, a question of degree in every case whether the judge is really legislating or not. Every decision worth consideration as a precedent of course carries the law a little further, but that is of the essence of case law, and indeed constitutes much of its merit. So far, that cannot fairly be called "legislation". The associated question, whether judges should refrain from giving rulings which really amount to legislation, can now no longer be answered unconditionally against such legislative activity, as it would in my view have been ten years ago by judges and lawyers generally, since it has been given a new and perhaps dangerous aspect, so far as the criminal law is concerned, in the case of Shaw v. Director of Public Prosecutions, [1962] A.C. 226. Before I go to a few of the cases earlier than Shaw, in which the judges could fairly be criticised as "legislating", I must give some consideration to that case, which was a criminal case, carried, as in exceptional cases criminal appeals may be, to the House of Lords. The case did not involve any class or political issue, and its importance lies in the scarcely disguised declaration by the House of Lords that the judges are at liberty, indeed under a duty, to legislate in certain fields.

The appellant in that case had published a periodical which was in effect a directory of prostitutes, with advertisements, and was prosecuted and convicted on three counts. The second and third of these, "living on the earnings of prostitution" and "publishing an obscene article", raise no point of interest for our purposes, but the decision of the House of Lords on the first count: "conspiracy to corrupt public morals", is very definitely of interest. (I explained the nature of the crime of conspiracy, and pointed out its dangers, at a little length in Chapter 2 of Book 1.) The prosecution based its case on the argument that there is a common law crime known as "corrupting public morals", and the Court of Criminal Appeal (as it was then called), from which the appeal was brought, held that this was so. The House of Lords, with the dissent of one very good judge, put the law only a little differently, holding that "conspiracy to corrupt public morals" is an existing crime. The serious matter, from our point of view, lies not so much in the ruling itself, but in the observations made by some of the judges, especially Lord Simonds, an able and vigorous judge of orthodox outlook, which could be very dangerous if they were applied to any class issue. Like all judges who are in reality legislating in their judgments, i.e., creating new crimes or new causes of action, he expressly disclaimed any intention of doing so:

"Need I say, my Lords, that I am no advocate of the right of the judges to create new criminal offences?"

But just before he said that, he had remarked:

"I am concerned only to assert . . . that such an offence [i.e., conspiracy to corrupt public morals] is known to the common law. . . . I must say categorically that, if it were not so, Her Majesty's Courts would strangely have failed in their duty as servants or guardians of the common law."

These words, whilst not in themselves stating that he was attributing to the courts a power to legislate, can only mean that it is part of the functions of the judges, as "guardians" under a duty to see to it that the common law should provide criminal sanctions for any conduct which seems to them to be outrageous enough to call for such sanctions, to rule and determine, when occasion arose, that such conduct was punishable as a crime even if no one had ever been indicted for it before. Lord Simonds went a good deal further, and showed still more clearly the duty he attributed to the courts, saying:

"I entertain no doubt that there remains in the courts of law a residual power to enforce the supreme and fundamental purpose of the law, to conserve not only the safety and order but also the moral welfare of the State, and that it is their duty to guard it against attacks which may be the more insidious because they are novel and unprepared for. . . . When Lord Mansfield, speaking long after the Star Chamber had been abolished, said, in the case of R. v. Delaval, in 1763, reported in 3 Burroughs, 1434, at p. 1439, that the Court of King's Bench was the *custos morum*—custodian of the morals—of the people and had the superintendence of offences *contra bonos mores*—against good morals—he was asserting, as I now assert, that there is in that Court a residual power, where no statute has yet intervened to supersede the common law, to superintend those offences* which are prejudicial to the public welfare. Such occasions will be rare, for Parliament has not been slow to legislate when attention has been sufficiently aroused. But gaps remain and

---

*For a court to "superintend" an offence can only mean that it will take cognisance of it and try and condemn citizens for it. Lord Simonds presumably used the word "offences" proleptically, as the context shows that he was ruling that the "residual power" enables the judges to make into *new* offences activities which are in their view "prejudicial to the public welfare". (There is of course no classification or subdivision in our law of existing offences into those "prejudicial to the public welfare" and others.)

will always remain, since no one can foresee every way in which the wickedness of man may disrupt the order of society.'

Then, after giving an illustration which plainly involved in certain circumstances that the courts ought to declare something to be criminal which had never before been treated as criminal, Lord Simonds added:

"Or must we wait until Parliament finds time to deal with such conduct?"

He wound up:

"I say, my Lords, that if the common law is powerless in such an event, then we should no longer do her reverence. But I say that her hand is powerful, and that it is for Her Majesty's judges to play the part which Lord Mansfield pointed out to them."

It is only too easy to see what dangers this sort of assertion of the right of the courts to legislate by way of creating new crimes can create in the political fields. There are not a few judges who are as genuinely horrified by Marxism as Lord Simonds was by profit-seeking pornography, and one can imagine, at any difficult moment, that one of them might say from his seat in Court:

"I entertain no doubt that there remains in the courts of law a residual power to enforce the supreme and fundamental purpose of the law, to conserve not only the safety and order but also the moral welfare of the State, and that it is their duty to guard it against attacks which may be the more insidious because they are novel and unprepared for. . . . There is in these courts a residual power to superintend those offences which are prejudicial to the public welfare"

and might go on from that to hold that to preach Marxism is "prejudicial to the public welfare", and thus an offence for which one does not have to await the activity of Parliament to fill the gap.

Of the four judges who sat in the House of Lords with Lord Simonds, one dissented, as I mentioned above, and the other three clearly agreed with Lord Simonds. I agree with the comments of Messrs. Ian Brownlie and D. G. T. Williams, two good Oxford University lawyers, who wrote in the *Canadian Bar Review* of December, 1964, that:

> "to decide *de novo* that a category of acts is to be the subject of criminal responsibility is to legislate on matters which should be within the scope of public debate and the pale of parliamentary law-making".

The Shaw case offers a good illustration of the dividing line between the useful and reasonable development of law by decisions and the more violent operations which can rightly be called judicial legislation. I will quote again from the scholarly article in the *Canadian Bar Review*:

> "The decision cannot be regarded as a further example of the technique of gently moulding the law by means of new definition of a well-established crime or a new application of recognised principles of the law of murder, larceny, forgery, or the like. The House of Lords and our other leading courts of criminal jurisdiction are declared to have the rights to enforce their opinions as to public morals by criminal sanctions."

I now come back, as I promised, to mention one or two examples of case law activities which amount, or nearly amount, to legislation, apart altogether from the extravaganza, if I may so call it, of Shaw's case, which is of course confined to the criminal law. Probably the most striking, and the one with the most obvious "class-conflict" flavour, is the invention of the doctrine of common employment, which I discussed at length in Chapter 15 of Book 1; almost equally striking is the resuscitation and extension of the tort of intimidation in the case of Rookes v. Barnard, dealt with in Chapter 11 of the same Book. Much more meritorious is the older example of the introduction of the "law merchant" into the common law, which I described earlier in this Chapter.

6

The Constitution

IT would be unthinkable to the lawyers of most countries that one could write an account of the shape and sources of the law of a country, as I have done in the preceding chapters, without discussing the Constitution of the country. Indeed, in most countries it would be dealt with in the first Chapter. But the Constitution of Great Britain has never been formulated in any document, and its position in the apparatus of our law is both typical of the formlessness of our law, and vividly illustrative of the methods of operation of our ruling class in the direct field of the class struggle.

If we are to examine what we have by way of a constitution, we must start by considering what, exactly, a constitution is. To lawyers in the U.S.A., in France, in any country of the British Commonwealth except Britain, in any socialist country, and in any state recently established, the Constitution is—and must be—a formal legislative document, enacted either by a special "constituent assembly" or by the country's parliament, making provision for such basic matters as the seat of sovereignty, the source of power, the powers of the parliament and its separate Chambers and of all the other organs of government, executive, legislative and judicial (to use the old-fashioned classification), the basic rights and duties of citizens, and perhaps other important matters, such as public and private property, rights to mineral and other natural resources, and of course provisions for the amendment of the Constitution itself.*

Britain has no such formal Constitution. Its informality

---

* In the case of socialist states, the Constitution may cover a good deal more. It may contain broad and magnificent political declarations as to the country's socialist basis and faith, of the human rights guaranteed to citizens and the means of their enforcement, and other such matters. Perhaps the best example of this is the most recent in date, the second Constitution of the German Democratic Republic, which came into force on 8th April, 1968.

would be quite impossible in any newly-established state, or in federal states, which by their very nature have to divide up the powers of government precisely and in detail between the federation and the constituent states. For example, Northern Ireland, a curious semi-sovereign state cut off from the rest of Ireland and preserved as part of the "United Kingdom" when the rest of Ireland became independent half a century ago, had to be given a written Constitution, which was enacted by the Westminster Parliament (as the Dominion of Canada and the Commonwealth of Australia had been dealt with in 1867 and 1900 respectively). But Britain, as I said, has no formal Constitution, and knows nothing of the distinctions drawn in most countries between laws which are part of the Constitution (and thus capable of amendment only by special machinery laid down in the Constitution itself) and laws which are called "ordinary". But our law, of course, deals in one way or another with all the matters that other countries cover in their formal constitutions, in the same way as we deal with such things as, say, contracts, although we have no code of contract law. And, for those who want to find and study our constitution, there is a long string of text-books, some long and some short, some scholarly and some not so good, in no sense official or authoritative but capable of guiding one to the provisions which deal with everything that other countries put in their formal documents. One can learn from these books, for example, of the unlimited legislative power of Parliament, which is a matter of common law; of the limitations on the powers of the House of Lords, which are laid down by statute; of the statutory provisions as to who may vote in elections to Parliament and as to the election procedures; of the statutory provisions that no Parliament may last for more than five years, and of the interesting piece of law—already mentioned in Chapter 4— that at any time Parliament, since it has absolute power of legislation, can validly provide by an ordinary Act of Parliament that the existing Parliament shall continue for more than the five years provided for by statute.

It is sometimes said that Britain has no Constitution, but it is not correct to say this without qualification. The real truth is that our Constitution—our legal expression of all the matters of law that normally form part of formal constitutions, and have the essential qualities that can be labelled as constitutional—is, like the rest of our law, formless but unquestionably present and effective. One can see in various official statements positive assertions of the existence of a Constitution. For example in relation to sedition, the most vaguely defined of all common law offences (with which I shall deal in a later volume), one of the heads of "seditious intent" which go to create the offence is "the intention to bring into hatred or contempt, or to excite disaffection against, the King, the government, and Constitution of the United Kingdom". Thus the case law—but not any Act of Parliament so far as I can trace—recognises that there is a Constitution, definite enough for an attack on it to create a criminal offence.

There is a more definite recognition of the existence of a constitution in the recent appointment of the "Commission on the Constitution", commonly called the Crowther Commission, the terms of reference whereof run:

"To examine the present functions of the central legislature and government in relation to the several countries, nations, and regions of the United Kingdom:

"to consider, having regard to developments in local government organisation and in the administrative and other relationships between the various parts of the United Kingdom, and to the interests of the prosperity and good government of Our people under the Crown, whether any changes are desirable in those functions or otherwise in present constitutional and economic relationships;

"to consider, also, whether any changes are desirable in the constitutional and economic relationships between the United Kingdom and the Channel Islands and the Isle of Man."

All the matters raised in these terms of reference are important, and can fairly be called "constitutional", and any measures which may have to be taken to implement the recommendations which the Commission may make will presumably have to take the form of legislation by the Westminster Parliament, the sovereign legislature of the United Kingdom, of a kind which in a country with a formal constitution would normally be dealt with by a Constitutional legislature. But there is nothing in all these matters which would lead to the creation of a formal written Constitution of the United Kingdom.

Our formless Constitution is part of the arsenal of the class war, and its very flexibility, like the flexibility of case law in general, which I discussed in Chapter 5, aids the ruling class in its cunning exercise of power. At any period of tension or of relative ease, it can operate with just the right degree of pressure to keep it safe in tension and avoid arousing unnecessary antagonism in quieter periods. I can best illustrate the practical working of this control by examining the position of what are called "basic rights" or "basic human rights", which in many formal constitutions are expressly set out, with the guarantees that are designed to safeguard them, thus imposing all sorts of restrictions on the activities of the ruling class, but which are unknown specifically to our own law.

By way of a detailed illustration, I will study fully one of these rights, that of public meeting or assembly, as it exists in our law. As I have just said, our law recognises nothing of the sort expressly, but our citizens nevertheless come off better than those of many countries where basic rights are expressly stated and guaranteed. Our legal basis for the existence and exercise of the right of public meeting, as for other similar rights, consists in the absence of any law rendering such activity unlawful as such, taken together with the attitude of the law that, if something is not unlawful, the citizen is free to do it. As there is no law prohibiting people gathering together and talking, or gathering together for one or more of them to talk to the rest, there is established—negatively, but effectively— a right of public meeting. But it is not a specially protected right and its reverse feature is that if, by or in the course of holding the meeting, one does break some law, or infringe the rights of some private person, one cannot rely on any "right of public meeting" to justify one's actions, and thus to render lawful what is otherwise unlawful. The legal difficulties with which holders of public meetings meet in practice lie in practical problems of where and how a meeting can in fact be held without infringing any law or private right. A meeting must be held somewhere. If it is to be held in a hall or other building, then the building must be hired from the public body or the private person who owns it, and—except for certain limited provisions applying only during and for elections—the owner is free to refuse to let the hall, without giving any reason.*

Thus there is no right to insist on the use of a hall. So, the open air? Even then, one must meet somewhere, and all the land belongs to someone, and he may refuse to allow it to be used. So, perhaps, one can try to use the street; but this is generally the property of some corporation, and even if it belongs to a private person his rights over it are limited. Thus, one has a chance. But the law still forbids one to obstruct the traffic, which has the primary and overriding right to use the street, and if the meeting does obstruct the traffic, the police may well insist that the street be kept clear, and thus in effect close the meeting, and if anyone refuses to move, asserting that he is not obstructing the traffic, the police will arrest him for obstructing *them* in the exercise of their duty. He can be only too sure that the magistrate will accept the police evidence as to what happened, and as to the fact that the traffic *was* being obstructed, so that it was their duty to tell the accused to move on. Thus, in effect, the meeting is stopped.†

It is curious, but surely accidental, that a legal right to make some use of the highway for purposes unconnected with the movement of traffic has been recognised by the Court in the case of Tynan v. Bolman, reported in the Law Reports, (1967) 1 Q.B. 91, and discussed in Chapter 12 of Book 1. There, the Court seemed to accept that the use of the highway for the exercise of the statutory right of "picketing", something wholly

* In 1933, when the unofficial but highly important and successful "Reichstag Fire Enquiry Commission" met in London, heard evidence, convicted the Nazis of having set fire to the Reichstag, and established that the Communists accused of doing so had had nothing to do with it, the then government of this country, "appeasing" the Nazis, played every trick it could to stop the Commission from functioning. One of these tricks was to try to prevent the use of any building for its sittings. It was foiled by the organisers having prudently hired a building from the Law Society (the official organisation of solicitors), with full disclosure of the reasons for hiring it. The Home Secretary, Sir John Simon, asked the Law Society to cancel the hiring, but was met with the reply that the contract of hiring had been made, with full disclosure, and that an official body of the legal profession could not flatly break its contract.

† I have often watched, in socialist countries—accused of being "police states"— policemen ordering people about, and being met with argument instead of obedience, and have reflected that, if they had offered even as much argument as that to British policemen, they would have been arrested and charged with obstructing the police and duly convicted and fined by the magistrates. If a "police state" is one in which the police can order people about with little or no resistance, then Britain is one; happily, in the more serious meanings of the phrase, it is not.

unconnected with the use of the streets for "passing and repassing", as lawyers phrase it, might be lawful.

Another, and perhaps a more frequent, way in which it may be alleged—and accepted by magistrates—that a meeting results in breaches of the law lies in what is said at the meeting. The statements of speakers may be said to be seditious, or to amount to "using insulting words and behaviour, likely to cause a breach of the peace". And people heckling at the meeting, sometimes protected or even encouraged by the police, may cause such uproar that the meeting can be closed down by the police, not in pursuance of any legal right to close, let alone prohibit, meetings as such, but on the ground that it is their duty to maintain order and that the only way to do so is to close the meeting. The net result of this is that the government, through the police and the courts, is in a position to disallow almost any exercise of the "right" to hold a public meeting when it feels the need to do so. And, with its usual cunning, the ruling class uses this advantageous position to earn itself a fairly good reputation, preventing any public demonstration which seriously inconveniences it and at the same time allowing every meeting which does not cause it anxiety. As part of this latter exercise of wisdom, it provides well-publicised safety valves like Trafalgar Square and "Speakers' Corner" in London and similar areas in provincial towns.*

The flexibility of the law makes it easy to "ride on the loose rein" when the general position in the country is quiet, and to act in the opposite way when things are difficult. In the 'thirties of this century, when slumps and heavy unemployment caused the ruling class great anxiety, the rein was tightened. Almost panic measures were taken to prevent public meetings being held in the streets in the neighbourhood of labour exchanges, where the unemployed were bound to congregate and to provide large audiences of people acutely conscious of employment difficulties. At the same period, on a larger scale, the police, on government directions, afforded large-scale protection to fascists who were violently attacking working-class people and thus acting as "lightning conductors". I need not deal in detail with these operations; they are too well known, and I

---

* Even in relation to Speakers' Corner, it required a great "civil rights" agitation a few years ago to prevent a realignment of the traffic routes in Hyde Park being used to get rid of practically all the speaking area.

dealt with them in my autobiography and also in a book which
I published anonymously in 1938, called *Justice in England*.
It is interesting today to re-read that book. Much of it, accurate
when it was written, is now only partly applicable because so
many minor reforms have been made in the generation which
has passed, but the essential strength of the ruling class and their
legal weapons has remained intact. It is true to say that the
decisions of the courts in the last seventy or eighty years, and
such legislation as the Incitement to Disaffection Act, 1934,
and the Public Order Act, 1936, have substantially diminished
the effective right to hold public meetings.

Returning to the general consideration of the formlessness
of the Constitution, it is a tribute to its flexibility and adapta-
bility as a weapon of the class struggle that it has enabled the
ruling class to ride through every constitutional crisis in our
long history with the minimum of legal difficulty. It is true
that in the seventeenth century we had an actual civil war,
but in the upheavals which followed it, including the replacement of the Stuart monarchy by "William and Mary", as well
as in earlier troubles like "Magna Carta" and later ones like
the dismissal of King Edward VIII, the constitutional arrangements involved were carried through without difficulty.

Formlessness brings another advantage to the ruling class,
namely that the Constitution, like the rest of the law, is relatively easily kept up to date through all the changes in the life
and economy of the people, and in the ruling class itself. We
suffer, for example, none of the difficulties which beset the
rulers, and the lawyers, of the U.S.A., where the exercise, and
sometimes the virtual destruction, of many of the rights of the
citizens of a vast monopoly-capitalist state have to be dealt
with in the framework of a Constitution drawn up nearly two
centuries ago by a ruling class of a few thousands of farmers,
traders and small industrialists, and amended from time to
time with few basic changes.*

---

* The rigidity of formal Constitutions is met in some of the socialist countries
by the introduction of new Constitutions at relatively short intervals.

7

The Judges

In ordinary parlance, the word "judge" includes anyone who hears and decides cases in the courts, but in England, by an oddity of current language among lawyers—and many laymen too—the word is generally confined to the few trained lawyers who staff the House of Lords, the Judicial Committee of the Privy Council, the Supreme Court of Judicature (comprising the Court of Appeal and the High Court of Justice) and the County Courts, whilst the many thousands of "Justices of the Peace", or magistrates who decide a thousand times as many cases—not all of them small ones—as do their more distinguished colleagues, are never called "judges".

The two groups, the judges and the magistrates, could not present a greater contrast, the first being highly trained and highly paid, and the second virtually untrained and virtually unpaid. I will deal with the judges in this Chapter, and with the magistrates in the next.

The judges are appointed from among barristers (a branch of the legal profession which I will describe in detail in Chapter 10), the usual requirement being fifteen years' standing. They are not elected. In a country whose leaders boast of its democracy, the very idea of the *demos*, the people, having any say in the selection of the judges who may have to deal with their grievances and their misdeeds and send them to prison, fills the establishment with horror—an unconscious revelation of our leaders' deep conviction that only a select, indeed a self-selected, few are fit to exercise any important function. Moreover, they feel that to keep all judicial appointments in their own hands does much to ensure that the whole apparatus of the law shall be absolutely reliable in any class-war emergency. I return to this point later in this Chapter. Of the judges, less than two hundred in all, the two dozen or so who hold the most important posts are appointed by the Prime Minister, and the rest by the Lord Chancellor. This important minister is always a lawyer. His position is anomalous, for on the one hand he is the head of all the judges, a body of men virtually irremovable and supposed to be wholly divorced from politics, and on the other he is an active politician, a Cabinet minister, appointed like all the other ministers by the Prime Minister, and liable to be dismissed at any moment. With any change of government he goes out automatically.

It seems odd, even to lawyers, that the most important judges should be appointed not by the Lord Chancellor but by the Prime Minister, who is not normally a lawyer and is not in charge of any legal department of the government. No doubt the Prime Minister in most cases takes the advice of the Lord Chancellor in making these appointments. But the power is deliberately given to the Prime Minister, and would be tenaciously defended if it were challenged, for two reasons. The first, and perhaps the least reprehensible, is that, however outwardly serene the establishment may appear, those in "the corridors of power" never forget that a serious challenge to their position and power may, indeed must, arise some time, and they will give up no right or power that may help them to meet it. They therefore keep the most important appointments in political hands, and not in those of a lawyer who might well make an appointment to a judicial post solely on the merits of the appointee as a lawyer, without regard to the attitude he would adopt to the establishment in a crisis. The political heads will prefer those who could be trusted to take the "right"—the tough—attitude in a crisis. The second reason, seen more obviously and frequently in practice, is that our ruling class has always attached the greatest importance to what it calls "patronage" and others call nepotism, i.e., the opportunity to help one's friends at the public expense, to provide a safe living for one's less intelligent relatives, and to reward one's political supporters and thus add to the numbers of those ready to support one.*

Patronage is, of course, a very old ruling-class game—and

* There is a story of one high minister saying to another: "Ceteris paribus [other things being equal] I believe in appointing my own political friends"; to which the other replied: "Ceteris paribus be damned."

weapon. In Chapter 2 of Book 1, in connection with the infamous Tolpuddle prosecution, I gave an illustration of the way in which the judge who tried the case had been appointed. There are many similar cases in more modern times. Of the many pretty scandalous exercises of patronage, quite a few— the top, it may be, of the iceberg—have become well known to the legal profession and to some extent to others, and only the workings of the law of libel (which I shall discuss in a later volume) has prevented them being made known to the general public at the time. Prime Minister Lloyd George supplies two samples. In one case, anxious to keep a second-rate politician, who was also a third-rate lawyer, in a minor post in his government for a time, he promised him a judgeship if he would stay on. The man did so, and when the time came for his reward Lloyd George asked the Lord Chancellor to make him a judge of the High Court, but the latter flatly refused, saying that the man was not fit for the post. It would have made too great a scandal to give him one of the higher posts that were in the Prime Minister's hands,* so the man finished up as a rather unsuccessful barrister. A more important and more scandalous example came also from Lloyd George; he had an Attorney-General of great ability and no principles, who coveted the then vacant post of Lord Chief Justice, which carried prestige, a high salary, and the blessings of irremovability, whereas Attorneys-General go out of office with all the other ministers when a government falls, and are not likely to get appointments from a government of another colour. The Attorney-General has what is loosely called a "right"—not of course legally enforceable— to claim any high legal appointment when there is a vacancy, but Lloyd George felt that this Attorney-General was indispensable as an able defender of the indefensible activities of his government, and persuaded him to stay in office for the time being, on a promise that he should become Chief Justice before the government went out. But how could they ensure that the office would fall vacant in time? They thought out and put into operation the following device. They appointed a "run-

---

* It is curious how even the worst of our leaders preserve some sense of outward decency (or fear of exposure) when "doing a job"; see the remarks of Lord Brougham, quoted in Chapter 2 of Book 1, in connection with the Tolpuddle case, and see too the quotation from Engels in the Introduction to the present volume.

of-the-mill" judge of the High Court to the post, ostensibly of course on the usual permanent basis, on his merits, but in reality as a sort of caretaker. And as such people as Lloyd George and his Attorney-General trusted no one, any more than anybody trusted them, they took from the caretaker a written and signed, but undated, letter of resignation, to be used when the imminent fall of the government or any other emergency arose, so that the Attorney-General could be free to take the coveted post. In due course, when the government was nearing its end, the letter was dated and the resignation announced in the press. The manœuvre was carried through so stupidly and brutally that the poor caretaker was not even told. The first he knew of it was when he read of his own resignation in his morning paper on a day when he happened to be in the middle of trying a long case. The Attorney-General, thus duly appointed, held office for many years, and was a notoriously bad judge. The whole sordid story was well-known to the general body of judges and barristers, and to the press, but the law of libel made it in practice impossible to tell it so long as the parties involved were still alive.

Two further, if less important, examples of the workings of patronage are worth relating. The first concerned the first Lord Halsbury, who was Lord Chancellor for many years, and was notorious for giving high office to his relatives. On one occasion he appointed an insignificant Tory M.P. a judge of the High Court, who dispensed injustice in that court for two decades. Lord Salisbury, the then Prime Minister, was heard to say: "Why has he appointed *that* fellow? They're not related." The other involved myself to a modest extent. I was addressing the House of Commons on some topic which concerned incidentally the appointment of judges, and I made a mild joke in the course of my speech about the evils of appointing people judges as a reward for political services. The joke was, to my mind, worth a smile or two, no more, but it was followed by a burst of loud laughter. I looked round to see why this should happen, and saw that a Tory M.P., notorious for busily pressing the Lord Chancellor to make him a judge, had just come into the chamber, thus giving point to my joke. Within a week, he was a High Court judge, but not a good one.

I should enumerate the courts in which the judges work.

D

Starting at the bottom, so to speak, there are the County Courts, created by statute early in the reign of Queen Victoria to bring civil justice within the reach, both geographical and financial, of those not too well off. They are oddly named in that they are not organised on a county basis, and their jurisdiction does not depend strictly on county boundaries. They have a limited but important jurisdiction. In general, the amount involved must not exceed £500. The judges are appointed from among barristers by the Lord Chancellor, and can be dismissed by him, but very seldom are. County Court judges can be promoted to the High Court, and from time to time are. Their courts are of great social importance, being to some extent "poor men's courts". Their procedure is simpler than that of the High Court, and the expense of litigating there is substantially less.

Then comes the High Court of Justice, the highest court of first instance, with unlimited jurisdiction. It is part of the Supreme Court of Judicature, and sits in three divisions, corresponding historically to the common law, equity, and the miscellaneous courts which dealt with admiralty, probate, and divorce. It has in fact criminal jurisdiction, although in London this is not immediately visible. The Assizes, at which all the more important of the major criminal cases outside London—those which cannot be dealt with at Quarter Sessions, a court which I will discuss in Chapter 8—are tried, are technically part of the High Court, as is the Central Criminal Court (the Old Bailey), where the corresponding criminal cases arising in London are tried. The Queen's Bench Division (common law) is presided over by the Lord Chief Justice, who is appointed by the Prime Minister; the Chancery Division (equity) is presided over in theory by the Lord Chancellor; and the Probate, Divorce and Admiralty Division has a President, who is appointed by the Prime Minister. All the other judges of this Court, called puisne judges, are appointed by the Lord Chancellor.

The Court of Appeal, the other part of the Supreme Court, is staffed by the Master of the Rolls and a number of Lords Justices of Appeal. They are all appointed by the Prime Minister. It hears appeals from the High Court and the County Courts, and it has recently been given jurisdiction to hear criminal appeals from Assizes, Quarter Sessions, and the Old Bailey, which formerly went to a Court of Criminal Appeal, staffed by High Court judges.

The House of Lords is the final appeal court from the Court of Appeal in England and from the highest courts in Scotland and Northern Ireland. Historically, this House, known primarily as the second chamber of the legislature, derives this appellate jurisdiction from the fact that it started life as part of the Magnum Concilium (great council) of the Kingdom of England, which dealt with judicial as well as legislative and to some extent executive matters in simpler days, before the conception of the separation of judiciary, legislature and executive had been developed. In theory, to this day, the House when hearing appeals consists of all the members, for the appeals are part of the business of the House; but in fact the only members who sit are the Lord Chancellor (when he has time to spare), a group of "Lords of Appeal in ordinary", who are lawyers appointed by the Prime Minister, generally from the Court of Appeal or the High Court, but occasionally from among barristers—they are made life peers in order to qualify them to sit—and then any judge or ex-judge of the Supreme Court who happens to be a member of the House of Lords.*

The origins of this court have caused practical difficulties. It does not matter very much that the judgments of the judges are in theory speeches in a debate, followed by a motion that the decision of the court below be affirmed, or reversed. But until quite recently, since the argument of a case was in theory the consideration of a petition presented by the appellant at the Bar of the House, the counsel arguing the case, who would seldom be less than four and might be far more, were cooped up with their papers and the numerous Law Reports which they would have to cite in a box which scarcely gave room for three of them, whilst their solicitors sat in equal discomfort on chairs outside the box. This has recently been remedied by the device of the House referring the appeals to a committee to hear and report. There the same judges, sitting as the committee,

---

* I was astonished one day, when arguing a case before the House, to see a peer who was not a lawyer stroll quietly into the Chamber, sit down near the Lords of Appeal, pick up a copy of the printed Record of the case which was being argued, look at it, take on an air of incomprehension, and then walk out. He was within his rights.

and the same counsel, can do their work in relative comfort in a committee room.

The Judicial Committee of the Privy Council is the final court of appeal from such countries of the Commonwealth as choose to permit such appeals, and from those colonies which still exist. It was until recently a very busy court, sitting generally in two divisions and occasionally in three, and spending much of its time hearing appeals from India before its independence. It is staffed by those members of the Privy Council who "hold or have held high judicial office", and a few others specially appointed under statutory powers. In practice, those who sit are members of the House of Lords "regular team", who are made Privy Councillors. Occasionally, members of the Court of Appeal, who are always made Privy Councillors, are borrowed, and there is some help from judges from the Dominions. This "Judicial Committee" has also an odd historical origin. As the old "plantations" became colonies, and grew in numbers and importance, and had to establish and staff courts with such skilled or semi-skilled personnel as they could find, more and more complaints arose of injustice perpetrated or alleged to be perpetrated by these courts, and as the law of each colony made no provision for appeals from its courts to any appellate body outside the colony, these injustices were made the subject of petitions by the parties aggrieved to the King, in a manner corresponding to the petitions, mentioned in Chapter 3, by which equity law was built up in England. The King referred these petitions to a committee of the Privy Council, which came to be called the Judicial Committee, for consideration and for advice to him as to what should be done with them. This Judicial Committee developed into a court which heard a gradually increasing number of appeals. It did not lead to the creation of a new body of law, as the petitions for equity had done, since the Committee confined itself to deciding what judgment should properly be given under the law prevailing in the colony involved.

In the case of the Privy Council, as in that of the House of Lords, the historical origin had some inconveniences. It did not matter much that in theory the judges were sitting as an advisory body to help the King to decide how to deal with the grievance of a colonial subject, and that their judgment had to take the form of an advice to the King. But it did matter that, until quite recently, when the practice was changed, the judges —advising the King—had to give him one specific piece of advice, their reasons for which had to be unanimous. In a case law country, the reasons of the judges, and their rulings, are of considerable importance to the body of law of the country, and often the judges, differing among one another as to what was the correct law, and having somehow to purport to agree with one another as to the advice they were giving and the reasons for it, were in real difficulty as to what they could say. The result was that the reasons were often obscure, that lawyers studying them for the purpose of arguing other cases were never sure as to what the more scholarly of the judges really thought, and some of the judges were indignant at having to appear to agree to reasoning which they thought to be wrong. In one case in which I appeared, I learnt that no less than seven drafts of a judgment, very different from one another, had gone to and fro between the judges before finally something could go out as the "advice" of the Committee. The final result was generally regarded by the profession as bad law!

The judges of the Supreme Court of Judicature can only be dismissed by a very complicated procedure involving the passing of a motion in each of the two Houses of Parliament.* This has never been done in relation to an English judge, and only once, long ago, in relation to an Irish one, but there have been one or two occasions when judges who have behaved badly have been quietly persuaded by the Lord Chancellor, or by their colleagues, to resign.

This virtual irremovability is one facet of the whole problem of the independence of judges, a matter of great importance. It is primarily designed to enable judges to ignore or resist any pressure, direct or indirect, from governments to decide cases in the way they desire, and this is plainly highly meritorious. The only influence that a British government could exercise today—and it would have to be done very discreetly—would be to hint that a decision in the High Court one way or another

---

* This provision is used in the House of Commons to frustrate M.P.s who seek to raise any question about the behaviour of a judge. The rule is that they may not raise the matter at all unless they are prepared to set down a motion for the dismissal of the judge.

would render it probable that the judge giving it would be promoted to the Court of Appeal or the House of Lords. There have been instances in which promotions have in fact followed important decisions, and the profession has thought that it saw a connection, but nothing of the sort has been demonstrable. And in any case any influence by way of possible promotion would not be very cogent, for the prestige, the work, and the rewards, as between one rank and another among the higher judges, are not greatly different. In countries where the judges are civil servants, and the grades which they can pass through in the course of, say, forty years of service are numerous, influence of this nature can be very strong. Certainly in West Germany, of which I have direct knowledge, the desire of the government for a particular decision can amount to positive direction, and we shall see, when I come to deal with the colonies in a later volume, where the judges are in the main removable, and the possible promotions are great both in variety and "differentials", that judicial independence is a mockery. I recall one case in which a judge of strong character and liberal outlook rejected influence from the governor of the colony, and caused a real sensation by doing so. A British subject who was no supporter of imperialism found himself in Ceylon, and gave a good deal of help to some Ceylonese against the government, which decided that he was a "trouble-maker" and must be run out of the colony. As he was a British subject, there was no legal means of achieving this end, so they adopted illegal means, and arrested him. He thereupon applied for a writ of *Habeas Corpus* (the traditional means of testing the legality of any detention). He had a quite clear case, and he did actually get his release, but when I came to read the judgment of the Chief Justice I found that it was very long and hesitant, and full of praise for the executive authorities, who had in fact behaved badly. I could not understand this, for at that time I had not so far had direct experience of colonial governments— of which in the end I had many mouthfuls!—and I knew the Chief Justice to be a lawyer of integrity and liberality. I had to wait some years for an explanation, which I got from him direct, as we were old friends. It appeared that the Governor, learning that the Chief Justice proposed to give judgment releasing the "trouble-maker", simply sent for him and *ordered* him to give judgment in the opposite sense, and was both surprised and angry when the Chief Justice refused. They had a stand-up row lasting a whole morning, but as the Chief Justice had the courage to stand firm the theoretical independence of the judges became real for the moment.

Judicial independence, which to English lawyers means in general the right of judges to decide cases as they think they should be decided, irrespective of the wishes of the government, and without disastrous consequences to themselves—which is best secured by making them virtually irremovable—is of course of great value, for it enables them to do justice as they see it (even if their eyes be sometimes astigmatic) fully and fairly in the teeth of the government and the establishment. (But I confess that I heard one day, to my astonishment, an able and upright judge of the Chancery Division express uneasiness at having had to decide a case against a government, although, he said, it was that very government that had appointed him a judge!)*

The principle became firmly established in England in the eighteenth century, when the new and rising middle class achieved success in its struggle against the power of the King as it had stood in the two preceding centuries; and it is now firmly established. (We shall see in Chapter 9 a similar and almost equally important struggle to achieve the independence of juries against the judges.)

The principle of irremovability has of necessity some disadvantages. To begin with, it tends to narrow the composition of the judicial bench, excluding many original or merely progressive minds from appointment, since irremovability leads the government—the Prime Minister or the Lord Chancellor, as the case may be—to select for appointment as judges only those on whom they can rely to accept and continue to accept, consciously or unconsciously, the establishment point of view. Then it has occasionally led to difficulties, as I have mentioned, when judges have acted unjustly, and it has been difficult to

---

* Judicial independence has different meanings in different countries. An old friend of mine, who occupied in France a position roughly equivalent to that of our Lord Chief Justice, told me once that he had always insisted proudly on his judicial independence. I wondered what he meant, and he explained that to him it meant that he retained and exercised all the political rights to which he was entitled as a French citizen.

get them out of office. Such difficulties are the price that has to be paid for the virtues of irremovability.

I should add that judges sometimes prove to be difficult in their relations with counsel (and vice versa!). The late Lord Buckmaster, who after he had ceased to be Lord Chancellor sat for long periods in the House of Lords and the Privy Council, was a sad example of what the French call "the defects of one's qualities". He was an outstandingly good lawyer, with a clear and very quick mind, and he unfortunately expected the minds of all who appeared before him to move at the same speed as his own. This was in fact impossible for nearly all of us, and he grew very impatient, often seeming to think that the judicial duty to "hear and determine" cases could be fulfilled by hearing little and determining swiftly. I once had to open and argue a complicated case before the House of Lords, over which he was presiding, and by mischance he had learnt that I estimated it would take a fortnight to argue. He was reluctant to believe that any case could or should last so long, and as soon as I began to open the case it seemed obvious that he had made up his mind to get rid of it quickly by one means or another. He began at once, with all the advantages of his quickness of thought, with a long series of interruptions. The system of interruption prevails in our appellate courts, and I was well accustomed to it. Indeed, I liked it, if it was not carried too far, for it helped one to know how the judges' minds were reacting. This time, the interruptions were so heavy that everyone present thought that he had resolved to "smash" the appeal, and waited with interest to see how I would react, for I was not accustomed to being "smashed", was highly conscious of my duty to see that my clients' case should be properly heard, and was not endowed with unlimited patience. The warfare went on for a day or two, and then Lord Buckmaster said: "Mr. Pritt, their Lordships"—that is the normal way of referring to the Court—"would like to know how long this *nonsense* is going to continue." I pulled myself together, made no complaint of a serious appeal being described as nonsense, and replied: "About ten days, if interruptions continue on their present scale, and a few days less if they diminish." This created an uneasy peace for a few hours. Then I responded to further and less endurable interruptions by slamming a book down on the little pulpit at which counsel then stood to argue, and shouting: "*Your Lordships are going to hear this case!*" This produced something of a shock, and a good measure of silence and attention from Buckmaster and his colleagues, and in a few days more I was able to convince them that I had a strong case which they could not throw out, and that they would have to hear the other side's arguments. Buckmaster, who bore me no malice, and had no intellectual defects save his impatient desire to decide cases quickly, called on the other side to argue, and proceeded to use on my opponent all the courteous brutality that had been previously shown to me. This he was probably doing merely because he had by then been persuaded that my appeal ought to succeed, and therefore wanted it to succeed as soon as possible. My opponent, destined himself to become Lord Chancellor and to display almost as much impatience as Buckmaster, actually crumpled under this treatment, and at the end of his argument, Buckmaster, impatient to the last, said to me: "Their Lordships will hear you in reply; but let me tell you that I have never yet heard a good argument in reply that took longer than a quarter of an hour." (I, personally, have known a reply to last a day, and win a case.) I accommodated him as far as I could, took twenty minutes, and in due course won the case. I relate this not as a good story, nor even primarily to show what barristers used to have to endure—I am told that the judges behave much better nowadays—but mainly to show what grave injustices the defects of even great judges can cause. My clients would not have been ruined if they had lost the case, but they had a perfectly good legal right to the money they were claiming, and they might have been poor men with an equally good case and a less stubborn counsel.*

In a later volume, I shall have to deal with a case which shows how bad a judge can be (and how the Privy Council tried to cover up for him).

I should write a few words about the relative merits of the

* I had a good friend in my student days who had his first case in court before a great judge who was almost as impatient as Buckmaster, and much less polite. He came out of court in a state of collapse, left the Bar, and became a very great colonial judge. And I had a pupil of exceptional gifts, who had a similar experience in one of his early cases, and asked me if counsel had to submit to such treatment. I replied that it was part of the price of success at the Bar to endure such treatment now and then. So he left the Bar and became the head of the legal department of the Foreign Office.

British system of appointing judges from among practising barristers and the system of the majority of capitalist non-Anglo-Saxon countries, under which the judges are civil servants appointed and trained as judges, never practising as advocates and moving slowly up the ladder of promotion from minor to major judicial posts. I have had a little direct experience of the latter system and of course long experience of the former. The latter system does facilitate government pressure for the judgment it desires, and the former enables both the judges and the advocates to understand one another better and to co-operate very well in the actual trying out of cases, but it is curious to reflect that British judges, entrusted with very difficult work, receive no direct training for it at all. The average judge, at the time of his appointment, will have spent at least twenty years, and often quite a bit more, as a barrister, conducting cases in which he appears for one side, bringing forward and emphasising everything that can be said on that side, and seeking to refute—and often under our elaborate procedure seeking to exclude altogether from consideration—what can be said for his opponent. He then becomes a judge, and with no more training or qualification than his probably substantial knowledge of the way cases work out in court, and how judges react to argument, he takes up in early middle age the wholly different task of hearing both sides, seeking to favour neither, remaining as indifferent as is humanly possible to the question which side is most meritorious or attractive, and finally deciding as impartially as possible on the facts and the law of the case. It is not surprising that judges occasionally behave like advocates. (When I first came to the Bar, one of the judges was a muddle-headed old man who had not been a very good advocate, and was not a very good judge, but had brought to the Bench all his partisan instincts as a high Tory. He had not been on the Bench very long when one of his old friends said to him: "Willy, I never realised that you were a good advocate until I heard you summing up that case to the jury yesterday.")

I must return for a moment to the question of bias in judges, on which I have already written something in this Book and in Chapter 5 of Book 1. Any accusation of bias in judges is highly emotive, and the defenders of the establishment maintain that judges are never affected by bias. This assertion ranks with the convention that all soldiers are brave, all lawyers learned, all priests saintly, all women virtuous, all editors of "national" newspapers independent, and all royal persons gracious. It is probably true that few judges are consciously and deliberately biased, in the sense that they will decide in favour of one side a case which they know that the other side ought to win, just because they dislike the politics or religion of one side. There have of course been a few clear and scandalous cases of bias, such as Tolpuddle, many less obvious cases, and countless cases in which it could well be suspected. But it is still true, to my mind, that in the majority of cases where judgments seem to rest on bias, the bias is unconscious, being nothing more than the necessary consequence of the judge's outlook, conditioned by his surroundings, of which I have already written.* I do not need to write more on it, except to give a small illustration, not of bias but of the distance which exists between classes, from the story of a judge who was trying a case in a Northern Assize Court. He asked a working-class witness at what time of the day some incident of which he was giving evidence had taken place. The man replied: "In t' dinner hour", and the judge was puzzled by the laughter in Court when he said: "Can't you be more definite than that? Dinner hour could be anything from seven to nine."

I should not leave this section dealing with courts without a few words about Courts-Martial, the courts which deal with charges, great or small, against serving members of the armed services. These charges relate for the most part to "service offences", contraventions of the many regulations covering the conduct of servicemen in their service, from serious charges like mutiny or desertion down to quite trivial matters, but they can also cover offences against the general law which applies to all citizens.

A Court Martial is a group of officers—not required to have any legal qualification or training—normally summoned expressly for the trial of a particular case or group of cases, and dissolved when it has been disposed of. They have the assistance of a legally-qualified officer called a "judge-advocate" (although

---

* The case of Liversidge v. Anderson, in which the majority of the House of Lords gave what many people think to have been a manifestly wrong interpretation of the war-time Regulation 18B, in what it held to be the war interest, could be regarded as a special variety of bias. I shall deal with it fully in a later volume.

he acts neither as a judge nor as an advocate) who advises them on points of law and sums up the case to them before they retire to consider their decision. In my experience, a good judge-advocate can transform a *prima facie* unsuitable tribunal into an almost good one. I need not discuss the procedure or the merits and demerits of Courts-Martial at length. Those who are interested can read my views in volume 2 of my autobiography, *Brasshats and Bureaucrats*, at pp. 236 to 269.

Until recently there were no appeals from decisions of Courts-Martial, but pretty full provision for their confirmation or non-confirmation by higher service authorities (who consider them in the absence of the parties), and for petitions by convicted men to the same authorities for review of convictions and sentences (considered in the same way). But relatively recently, largely as a result of some of the cases which I related in *Brasshats and Bureaucrats*, a genuinely judicial procedure of appeal to judges of the Supreme Court, sitting as "the Courts-Martial Appeal Tribunal", was established by the Court-Martial Appeals Act, 1951 (14 & 15 Geo. 6, c.46), subsequently amended in 1964 and 1966.

8

The Magistrates

As I mentioned in the preceding Chapter, the "Justices of the Peace"—whom I shall call by their more usual name of magistrates—present an extreme contrast to the professional judges of the higher courts.

As an institution, the magistrates are many centuries old. They have always been unpaid until quite recently, since when they receive a small sum designed to cover their expenses. Until a few years ago they received no education or training for their work, since when those newly appointed are given a very little. They sit part-time only. In large cities, where the volume of work calls for continuous sittings, they are wholly or partly replaced by paid professional magistrates, called stipendiaries, whom I shall discuss later in this Chapter.

Until a little over a century ago, the magistrates were entrusted not only with judicial functions, but also with most of the not very elaborate work of local administration and with the maintenance of law and order. Today, they confine themselves to judicial work, in which in their thousands they deal with a great volume of work, which I will describe below. Included in this is the important function of granting—or refusing—warrants for arrest or search on applications made to them by the police in private and in the absence of the persons concerned. There have been instances of the police finding some magistrates very easy-going in such matters, and consequently resorting to those magistrates all the time. In one notorious case a warrant which ought not to have been granted was found to have been granted by a magistrate who was 101 years old! (Today they give up work at 70.)

In theory the magistrates are still under a duty to maintain law and order in emergencies, but in practice the central government and the police forces, with in rare cases the armed forces, deal with the matter.

The magistrates have always been important and orthodox local people, who can be relied on to follow the views of the establishment in all their work. Their composition has naturally varied through the centuries. The present method of their appointment is elaborate. It is not laid down by any Act of Parliament, and although it would be an exaggeration to call it secret, successive governments show no readiness to give solid information about it. It is simple enough on the face of it. They are appointed by the Lord Chancellor in the name of the Queen. But whence does the Chancellor get the necessary material on which to exercise his judgment? He receives recommendations from "Advisory Committeees", themselves magistrates, in each county;* and these committees prepare their recommendations on the basis of lists submitted to them by the three main political parties—Labour, Conservative, and Liberal—thus ensuring that nearly all the magistrates are or have been active in party politics of an establishment flavour (and of course the members of the Advisory Committees, being magistrates, are themselves the products of earlier operations of this "list" system). What nobody knows is how often the Chancellor appoints persons who have not been so recommended, or refuses to appoint persons who are, but it is generally believed that the great majority of those appointed are those recommended. The only well-authenticated piece of evidence on the point comes within my personal knowledge, and relates to an acquaintance of mine whom Lord Chancellor Birkenhead wanted to appoint. Birkenhead did not simply appoint him straight off, but asked the Advisory Committee for the County involved to recommend him. It refused to do so, and he then threatened that, if it did not do so, he would appoint the man "off his own bat". That this very imperious Chancellor went through that elaborate procedure, instead of simply making the appointment that he wanted to make, is a strong indication that at any rate in his day recommendations of the Advisory Committees were pretty well equivalent to

---

* Counties are still important in many ways. There are many survivals in our governmental apparatus from the days when almost all administration was based on the counties, and not on the centre.

appointments, and that the absence of recommendation was not lightly to be by-passed. Thus, one can be almost sure that any magistrate before whom one's case may come, who is supposed to be non-political, has been in effect made a magistrate by one or other of the three main parties on the basis, at any rate in part, of his political activities or affiliations.

No one is likely to be recommended for appointment unless he is known to be willing and able to give up to it, on an average, one day a week, and thereby to lose roughly a day's earnings if he is "gainfully occupied". One can be equally sure that no one will be recommended unless the necessarily orthodox-minded Advisory Committee regards him or her as "safe" from an orthodox point of view. The modern development of public opinion has ensured, especially in industrial areas, that a certain number of members of the Labour Party, including working-class members, are appointed, but, on economic as well as political grounds, they will come mainly from among the better paid, the elderly, and the retired, who can afford to give time to the work, and, in terms of numbers, they will tend to be relatively few.

Apart from these special considerations, it must seem curious that enough people are ready to do, without pay, the rather difficult and often dull work of "hearing and determining" cases, but so far there have always been enough would-be magistrates to fill the vacancies (although one hears complaints of the intellectual qualities of those available). One reason for the readiness to do the work is basically a "snob" one, namely that the label of "J.P." still carries a good deal of social prestige. This actually makes the political element in recommendations a more serious defect than it might otherwise be, for it is inevitable that ambitious minor politicians will be actually pressing their party organisations to secure recommendations for them to what one scornful critic called the "knighthood of the underlings". The readiness to clamour for one's own snob-advancement—or even the taking up of political activity to that end—is no proof that one will make a good judicial officer.

Then, when magistrates are appointed, what work do they do, how do they do it, and how do they learn—so far as they do learn—to do it? Taking the last point first, the position up to

a few years ago was that no one taught them anything about
the law, the procedure, or the rules of evidence, let alone the
necessity to avoid bias, or rumour, or what they had heard
outside the court, and to decide simply on the evidence brought
before them in court, or any other of the many difficult disciplines and requirements of judicial work. They simply "picked
it up as they went along";* and if accused persons came before
magistrates whose ignorance of their professional duties led
them to convict the accused without sufficient evidence, or on
evidence that they should never have admitted, or on "facts"
the magistrates had heard outside, or even on the belief that
the accused were Communists, they had to put up with the
injustice unless they could afford to appeal, and if they appealed
their case would come before a Court of Quarter Sessions
staffed by other magistrates appointed and "trained" in the
same way. In the course of modern "tinkering" with the defects
of the system—often good tinkering, but never more than
tinkering, with the fundamental defects of the system left
untouched—it has recently been arranged that newly-appointed
magistrates, and only these, should be given some brief preliminary training for their work. When one remembers that our
law, our procedure, and our law of evidence are so complicated
that a newly-qualified barrister who has spent three years or
more in intensive study and then passed some very difficult
examinations is universally regarded as not capable of conducting even a simple case unless he has also spent a year as a
pupil in the chambers of an experienced barrister in order to
learn how to do his work, one may be sceptical as to how far
this preliminary training of laymen may help to fit them for the
more responsible work of deciding cases.

What work do the magistrates do? It is not unimportant or
occasional, but covers in one way or another the whole of the
criminal law. It is all criminal, save for a few little bits of civil
law which, whilst not socially unimportant, are of too small a
volume to call for consideration here. As for their criminal
work, it comes into both the two main sections into which our

* One can imagine what a mess laymen can make of our elaborate legal procedure, as lawyers might make, say, of an engineering job. I was once driven by
exasperation to tell a chairman of a country bench of magistrates, who was a
colonel, that he was as fully equipped to try a case as the solicitor appearing before
him, who was doing his best to make him try the case properly, was to command a
battalion.

procedure divides the cases, viz: the small charges that can be and are disposed of in one court, the magistrates' court, "at one go", and the other more serious charges, called indictable because they come to trial before a superior court, before a jury, and are preceded by a formal accusation called an indictment, after a previous investigation before the magistrates. For convenience, I shall sometimes describe the two types of procedures as "major" and "minor".

In major cases, the actual trial, in most countries, is preceded by some form of judicial enquiry designed both to ensure that these cases shall only be carried to trial when preliminary investigation shows that there is a substantial case to be tried, and that the case shall be properly prepared, in particular in the sense that the accused gets adequate and timely knowledge of the charge he has to meet.

In England, minor cases are tried before the magistrates, sitting without a jury (but with at least two magistrates), in courts which are held in nearly every town, including quite small ones. These are officially called "petty sessional courts", but normally magistrates' courts or police courts. Subject to what I have to say later about stipendiary magistrates, all minor cases—of which there are hundreds of thousands every year—are tried and disposed of by the untrained magistrates (with a right of appeal, as I have said, only to other magistrates in Quarter Sessions, apart from pure questions of law, where there is a complicated procedure enabling the point to be carried to the High Court).

Nor are the magistrates confined to the minor cases. Every major case, which if it comes to trial will be heard before a jury at either Quarter Sessions—which I will describe later—or at the Assizes or the Central Criminal Court, must start with the judicial enquiry mentioned above, which takes the form of a public hearing of evidence before the magistrates. This proceeding, which to a layman seems indistinguishable from a full trial, is essentially different from a trial because it is not used to determine guilt or innocence but only to decide whether the evidence produced by the prosecution makes out a case sufficiently substantial to call for a trial, in which event the magistrates send it—technically, "commit" it—to a higher court for trial.

E

I should mention that, in respect of a large number of major charges, the magistrates have jurisdiction in certain circumstances to deal with them as if they were minor charges. Reverse-wise, in many minor cases the accused can insist on the case being treated as a major one. I shall return to this in Chapter 9.

Thus, we can see that every criminal charge, major or minor, comes before the magistrates, either for actual trial or for investigation and eventual committal.* But even that is not all the work of the magistrates, for when a case is committed for trial it goes either to the Assizes (or in London to the Central Criminal Court), or to the Quarter Sessions. If it goes to the Quarter Sessions, magistrates, sitting as judges of that court, will deal with it there too. A small list of particularly grave crimes are triable only at Assizes or the Central Criminal Court, and all other major crimes—although for convenience they may go to Assizes or the Central Criminal Court—go to Quarter Sessions. There they come before a bench of magistrates, the chairman of whom will have to sum up to the jury, explaining to them the law which he is not required to know. The full horror of this has of recent years been much reduced by more tinkering, consisting in the appointment of barristers and occasionally judges to act as such chairmen. This is of substantial help, of course, for these professionally qualified chairmen can at any rate rule on points of evidence and sum up the case to the jury, but if the Quarter Sessions are busy the court may sit in two or even three divisions, and the chairmen of all but one division may well be untrained lay magistrates.

Having described the work of the magistrates, and seen some of their difficulties, I come to the question: how do they do their work? The truthful answer is: "Badly." One could also say: "Not nearly as badly as might be expected." But that is still: "Badly." In dealing, on minor charges, with questions of fact, they are no worse, and no better, than any other group of laymen making a decision on a bunch of half-known facts and impressions, with a good deal of bias, and with little notion of the duty of courts to decide judicially on the evidence. It is often said in their defence that they learn by experience. So

---

* There are very rare exceptions to this rule, perhaps one case in a few million, but we need not concern ourselves with them.

they do, but in effect they learn by experience of doing things badly to do them badly, if a little more quickly.

In dealing with matters where prejudice—political, social, industrial, or moral—comes into play, they inevitably apply the "safe" outlooks which led to their being appointed, and do not make efforts which most professional judges make, with varying success, to pay regard only to the proved facts and the applicable law. Why should they make these difficult efforts? No one has done much to teach them to do so, or even to tell them to try.

One could give many instances, both in large and in small cases, of the inevitably biased fashion in which magistrates work in cases when political or other prejudice is involved. We have certainly progressed from the not very distant days when all the magistrates in a rural area were landowners who preserved game, when most of the cases that came before them were charges of poaching, when every alleged poacher was convicted and heavily punished, and when the magistrate who actually owned the land on which the poaching was alleged to have taken place would move a yard along the Bench and explain that he was not adjudicating in that particular case. (When the next case came on, he would move back into his seat, and one of his colleagues would move a yard.) But while we have made progress, one could, as I say, give many instances of unsatisfactory work. I will confine myself to one, in which I happened to be professionally engaged.

In the Autumn of 1937 at a time when some magistrates and a good many other people were not only prejudiced against even mildly left-wing people but actively in favour of fascists, a civil servant whom I later came to know pretty well—a man of intelligence and integrity, a member of the Labour Party, with a distinguished record in the First World War—was prosecuted in a magistrates' court in Surrey under the Official Secrets Act for "retaining information" and for "not taking proper care of information", involving three documents with which he was lawfully concerned in the course of his duties. The matter arose in this way: he was employed in the Royal Aircraft Establishment at Farnborough and lived in a bungalow not far from it. At times, like many civil servants in similar work, he had in his possession papers containing notes or information relating to his work which, strictly, he should not have left in his bungalow. The matter was trivial enough for *The Aeroplane*, hardly a left-wing publication, to have written of it afterwards: "There can hardly be a junior draughtsman or a member of a technical department in the Aircraft industry . . . who could not be prosecuted and convicted . . . on a precisely similar charge."

Whilst the man was away on his summer holiday, leaving his bungalow unoccupied, four young men, some of whom said that they were fascists, and one of whom was an army deserter, burgled the bungalow and removed from it a quantity of clothing, cutlery, money, a watch, a telescope, and some of the papers I have mentioned. They were caught by the police and prosecuted for theft, being defended at the Surrey Quarter Sessions by a barrister who was a fascist. The defence was that the civil servant was a Communist, and that the thieves were patriotic citizens who had raided the bungalow in order to secure the papers and report the matter to the authorities. That they had taken a good deal of property other than the papers was thus explained by two of them: "We just jumbled everything into the cases." As the *News Chronicle* described it, the case "was so conducted that Mr. —— appeared to be in the dock and the thieves almost assumed the role of prosecutor. Mr. ——'s character was blackened and his prospects in life jeopardised by what appears from the reports to have been a flagrant violation of the laws of evidence."

That is how the magistrates in Quarter Sessions allowed the case to be conducted. But the jury did not accept the story, and convicted the four men. The court released them, however, merely "binding them over" to be of good behaviour for twelve months.

The civil servant had meanwhile been suspended from his duties. This treatment, in the atmosphere of that pre-Munich period, was not as incredible as it would have appeared ten years earlier, or ten years later. When the unfortunate civil servant was prosecuted as I have stated above he employed in his defence the great left-wing solicitor W. H. Thompson. Thompson thought that, in that atmosphere, and as the man had on the very wide words of the Official Secrets Act clearly committed a technical offence, the best course was for his client to plead guilty. He then decided that I should represent the man, and make the necessary explanation and exonerations—what is called "the speech in mitigation". I was sure that I was not the right man for the job, but Thompson overruled me, and we went down to the court. The magistrates looked pretty hostile, and with Thompson's warning about the atmosphere and the habits of country magistrates in my mind, I wondered what sort of a sentence they were going to inflict on my client for an offence for which a fine of 20s. would have been more than enough. The result was a fine of £50, a large sum in those days. As we left the court, I said to Thompson: "Well, did I do any good, or would he have been fined that much anyway?" The tough Thompson replied with one of his rare tributes: "You don't know country magistrates as I do. I was watching them all the time. They were listening to you, and I was saying to myself, in a sort of Dutch auction: 'They want to give him six months—Pritt's got them down a bit—down to three months —down to one month—they're not going to send him to prison after all—they'll fine him £100—it's down to £50.' And then you stopped, and they said £50. You couldn't have got them further."

Magistrates are obviously not very skilled in dealing with questions of law, which arise before them constantly, both on the common law and on the interpretation of innumerable Acts of Parliament, not always well drafted, and also on questions of admissibility of evidence, often very difficult and very important. When a point of law, great or small, arises, the barrister or solicitor who has to argue it addresses the magistrates, in as simple English as possible (there is no harm in that) cramped by the knowledge that at the best they will only understand half of what he is saying, that they want to finish the case and go home or to their business, and that the natural tendency of courts is to want to decide the question, whatever it is, in the way, right or wrong in law, which will help the side which to their minds has the merits of the case in a lay sense. The virtual hopelessness of such a position is alleviated in practice by the fact that every magistrate's court is attended by a "clerk to the justices", who is at any rate a trained lawyer, generally a local solicitor. He has no judicial or magisterial status, but the magistrates are entitled to consult him, and to get his professional opinion on the questions of law they have to decide. Often, if they retire to their private room to dicuss what they should decide, he retires with them. The whole system is indefensible from any orthodox legal point of view, for it amounts to having the judicial work of a court, which is in fact incapable of doing it, done behind the scenes by someone who is capable of doing it but has no status or position entitling him to do it. In practice, the system doesn't work too badly. It varies greatly from court to court, some justices' clerks being extremely good, and others moderate, and some magistrates being more ready than others to accept the clerks' advice. In the actual work of barristers and solicitors, the anomalous position is not easy. In some courts, where the magistrates stand on their dignity and pretend they know their job, one has to be careful to address one's arguments to them, without looking at the clerk but in the confidence that he is listening. Then the magistrates and the clerk will retire, and one at any rate knows that there is someone there who has listened to the arguments and knows what the question is. In other courts, where the clerk is a strong personality, and the magistrates do not worry so much about "face", one can—whilst apparently addressing the magistrates—in reality address the clerk, who sits just below the chairman. And the interruptions from the bench, which form an important part of the proceedings in the higher courts, and are not unknown in lower ones, may even be made directly by the clerk. I remember once, in a magistrates' court near London, listening to an able and not particularly humble solicitor, who did not often appear in that court and thus did not feel the need for any especial tact, arguing a point with frequent interruptions not only from the clerk but from a young and vigorous assistant of the clerk, who was sitting by his side. When the solicitor had had enough of this, he ostentatiously lifted his gaze up to the chairman, and asked: "Could I have your direction, sir, as to whether I am to argue this point of law with your learned clerk, or with your learned clerk's clerk?"

Sometimes, especially in sparsely-populated districts, where lawyers are "thin on the ground", this system may have serious defects. Solicitors who act as clerks to justices are nearly always engaged on a part-time basis, and give most of their time to their private practice as solicitors, naturally in the same district. Accused persons who see the same person advising the justices on their rulings in a case brought against him by the police, and spending much of his time in a neighbouring court conducting cases on behalf of the police, may well feel aggrieved. In one extreme case which came to my notice, the clerk actually called and examined the witnesses for the prosecution, advised the magistrates on the admissibility of disputed evidence, accompanied them when they retired to consider whether they should commit the accused for trial, and then—when he had been committed—acted as solicitor for the prosecution to prepare the Brief and to "instruct" a barrister to prosecute at Quarter Sessions.

I must write something about the important duty of magistrates when dealing with major cases which the prosecution desires to have committed for trial. They have to make up their minds whether the case is strong enough. To make such a decision calls for real skill and experience in the weighing of evidence. It may call, too, at times for some courage, when the prosecuting authorities obviously very much wish the accused to be committed for trial, but the evidence is not strong. The temptation for unskilled laymen, accustomed to co-operate with the police—and to accept the evidence of police witnesses— is to say to each other: "Well, it's not a strong case, but the prosecution won't like it if we throw it out, and a man whom *they* think guilty will get off. Let us send him to trial. If after all he has a good defence the jury can acquit him." Thus quite a number of cases go to the Assizes or Quarter Sessions, where the judge or the chairman directs the jury to acquit, and may even say that he cannot understand how the case was ever sent for trial. Meanwhile, much labour, time, money, and anxiety have been spent on the case.

Magistrates, through their contact with the police and the prosecuting authorities, tend to become what lawyers call "prosecution-minded". Whilst it is their duty to decide all questions between the police and the prosecution authorities on the one side and the accused on the other with complete objectivity, weighing the evidence on its merits, they have in most courts a strong tendency to make orders which the police ask for (especially on questions of releasing accused men on bail, where the police often want to keep them in custody, not because there is any fear of their disappearing but in order to spend hours "interviewing" them—occasionally, too, because they want in effect to punish them by keeping them in prison for a week or two for offences for which, even if they are in the end found guilty, they would only be fined and not imprisoned), and also to accept the evidence of police officers even when there is grave doubt of its reliability. I recall one extreme case (not as it happens of a lay magistrate) of a London stipendiary, whose practice as a barrister had mainly been confined to conducting prosecutions, saying bluntly to a solicitor—on the *first* day he sat as a magistrate after his appointment: "If you are asking me to disbelieve the police evidence, you are wasting your time."

The question naturally arises: why is this amazing system allowed to continue, in a country where the law and the courts enjoy great prestige as the one secure resort for just treatment of the citizen, and where the most trivial civil case has to be tried by professionally qualified judicial personnel? There are a good many reasons, varying in strength. It is not really cynical to give, as one reason, the fact that the system is there, and has been there for a long time, for the "establishment" always resists fundamental change, and seeks to head off criticism by "tinkering" reforms. The system can be kept going so long as sufficient people can be found to staff the courts, which as I have mentioned is still the case, and it is an advantage from the ruling-class point of view that the great majority of those who can spare the time for such work are just the sort of "establishment-minded" people they want. It is thus easy to secure convictions in cases having any odour of politics or protest. Another reason is that the system is very cheap in administrative costs, as the magistrates are virtually unpaid, and any imaginable replacements would have to be well-paid. Moreover, at any rate until quite lately, the sufferers from the poor quality of magistrates' work have been drawn from the working class, and not from those whose complaints are more easily ventilated and make more appeal to the ruling class. Today, with people from all classes being charged with motoring offences, and with so much political agitation bringing all sorts of people into contact with the police and the magistrates, this position has altered to some extent, but not yet sufficiently to create a swelling demand for reform of the magistracy. (And why should the ruling class take steps to give the mass of the working class good justice, when they do not give them good housing, food, or medicine?)

It is only fair to say that one reason for the continued maintenance of such an unsatisfactory system is that it is not easy to find a satisfactory remedy in present circumstances. At first sight, it seems clear that what is required is a staff of professional magistrates, either barristers or solicitors, as has always been done in colonially-governed territories, as for example Ireland before liberation, and India, where sufficient lay magistrates could not easily be found, and would in any case not be "safe" from a ruling-class point of view. But the already fairly full experience of the work of stipendiary magistrates in London and other large cities has not been encouraging for those who would like to see this remedy adopted. With one or two distinguished exceptions, the stipendiaries have proved to be rather more orthodox and "prosecution-minded" than lay magistrates, and further from understanding what "makes the ordinary citizen tick". Thus, one would get from this reform nothing more than greater efficiency, and no improvement in quality. Reform will not be simple until the legal profession, which I shall discuss in Chapter 10, has become much more progressive.

Looking at the whole picture, I think that perhaps the strongest reason why the system still remains almost intact is that it is pre-eminently "safe" from the ruling-class point of view. It is a "built-in" safeguard against really just consideration being given to any activity or policy unwelcome to ruling-class minds, be it trade unions, strikes, peace, or anti-racialism.

In conclusion, I must say something about Recorders, and professional chairmen of Quarter Sessions. Recorders are barristers appointed to preside at Quarter Sessions in certain cities and boroughs, where they do the work which in counties is done by the magistrates. In a few large towns, they work whole-time, giving up their practices at the Bar, and are well paid. They are in effect minor judges, but in most towns they sit only once a Quarter and then only, in general, for a few days, and they are mostly poorly paid. Some barristers like to have such appointments for prestige or snob reasons, and also because they think it may help them after a time to secure appointments as High Court judges.

The paid professional chairmen of Quarter Sessions are barristers, appointed as magistrates to give them the necessary qualification to sit. In London and one or two counties, there is enough work for the Quarter Sessions to do to justify these chairmen in giving up their practices and becoming whole-time and well-paid judges, like the recorders of large towns. But for the most part they sit part-time and continue with their practices. The employment in this way of professional chairmen is a good example of "tinkering", for the chairman will in reality, although not in theory, rule on all questions of evidence and all other questions of law, and will sum up the case to the jury. These are tasks which are very important in courts which try serious major cases, but, as I mentioned above, there is always the risk that, if a court sits in more than one division at a time, an accused person may find his serious case being tried before a jury of twelve laymen, presided over by three or four lay magistrates, one of whom will sum up the case to the jury, and direct them as to the law.

None of the "tinkering", of course, changes the class outlook of the court.

9

Juries

THE jury system provides interesting material in connection with the class war. I will first state the legal position and the actual operation of the system, and then consider the class-war implications and the measures taken by the ruling class to deal with the dangers that may arise from the intrusion of this substantial lay element into the work of deciding cases.

The jury is today an essential part of the administration of the criminal law, since the courts entitled to try major cases must sit with a jury of twelve laymen who alone can find the facts and declare the accused guilty or not guilty. (Juries are important, too, in civil cases. I will discuss this a little later.)

Originally the jury was a body of an indefinite number of people in each county, likely to know what was going on in their area, who were called upon to report to the King's judges when they travelled round the country "on circuit" to try cases of crimes alleged to have been committed in the county since their last circuit. In the course of time the jury has been completely transformed into a group of—normally—twelve persons called to sit in court, hear the cases, and return their verdict. It is essential, since they have to decide on the evidence brought before the court, that they should know nothing about the case before they start their work. (This is not always easy, since in cases with "news-value" the preliminary proceedings before the committing magistrates will have been widely reported, but the real evil of this has been largely cured in recent years by restrictions on the reporting of committal proceedings.)

In court, the jury sit in an enclosure, called a "box", separate from the judge, and listen to the whole case—the opening speech of the counsel for the prosecution (or, in civil cases, for the plaintiff), to the evidence of the witnesses for both sides, the closing speeches of counsel (or, where an accused is not defended, the accused himself), and finally to the "summing up" of the judge, in which he tells them the law governing the case, and—in all but very simple cases—reminds them of the substance of the evidence. He may hint or suggest to them how they should assess the evidence of one witness or another, and indeed how they should decide the whole case, so long as he makes it clear to them that all the questions of fact are a matter for their decision alone, that they are indeed the judges of the questions of fact. (It is often amusing to listen to a strong-minded judge doing his best to get from a jury the verdict he wants. Juries generally follow his suggestions, but occasionally react adversely and return the opposite verdict.) When the summing-up is concluded, the jury consider their verdict, retiring to their private room if necessary, and then return to court and give it publicly. On all questions of law, the judge alone decides, and they must accept what he tells them. In criminal cases, this arises generally in the business of telling the jury what has to be proved to constitute guilt in the accused, but the rule applies equally to any question of law that arises in the course of the case.

The summing-up is very important, and the judge must take care to explain the law clearly and accurately, lest a man who is probably guilty should, after the jury have found him guilty, escape on appeal because the judge stated the law wrongly to his detriment, and the Court of Appeal holds that it is not safe to let the verdict of guilty stand (and it should not be forgotten that, however important it is that innocent men should not be found guilty, it is also important that the guilty should not escape!). The obvious remedy for such a mishandled trial would be to order a new trial; but English law has always stood strongly by the principle that a man should not be tried twice for the same offence. But quite recently, by the Criminal Appeals Act, 1968, a narrowly-limited power to order new trials has been granted. The right arises only where the Court of Appeal, when allowing an appeal against a conviction, does so only by reason of some evidence received or available to be received by the Court of Appeal. (Normally, the Court of Appeal does not hear evidence, for all the evidence should be heard before the jury at the trial, but it is specially empowered by this new Act to order any witness who would have been a compellable witness at the trial—"compellable witnesses" are those who are bound by law to give evidence if they are called on to do so; normally, everyone is so compellable, but there are some exceptions, especially in the case of the wives of accused men—to attend before the Court of Appeal and give evidence there. In that very narrow but not unimportant field, the Court of Appeal may, if it appears that the interests of justice so require, order a new trial of the case. But even then the power is limited, in that the new trial can only be for the offence of which the appellant was convicted and in respect of which the appeal is being allowed, or for an offence of which he could have been convicted on the original trial for that offence—there are many cases in which an accused, charged with one offence, can be convicted of another similar (and generally smaller) offence—or for an offence with which he was charged at the trial as an alternative, but of which he was not convicted because the jury was discharged from giving a verdict thereon if they convicted him on the first offence.*

At times, of course, cases are so simple that very little summing-up is needed. There is a well-authenticated case of an obviously hopeless civil case, with an element of blackmail in it, where a judge and a very alert jury had to listen for over an hour to what they could all see was a swindle. As soon as the plaintiff's counsel had finished his final speech, the summing-up by the judge consisted in his silently turning to the jury and raising his eyebrows, whereupon the jury, thus adequately "directed", returned a verdict for the defendant.

The jury system is today rather less important in civil cases. For centuries, a civil case, like a criminal one, could only be tried with a jury,† but for a long time before the present century began it was possible, if the parties wished, to have a "non-jury" trial. This was often done in long and complicated cases, or those involving a great deal of technical evidence. (But sometimes, even in such a case, one party would often insist on a

* This often happens; an instance of it can be seen in the Liverpool and London Dockers' trial related in Book 1, at pp. 93–96.
† This did not apply in the equity courts, which never had juries, and often had the facts dealt with by affidavit, or—in cases with difficult questions of fact—would direct the issue to be tried in a common law court (and thus with a jury).

jury, thinking that the jury would be more likely to decide in its favour. I remember a long case relating to electrical supply being so tried, in which the plaintiff's counsel, a lively and rather theatrical advocate of great ability, began his final speech thus: "Gentlemen of the jury, what do you and I care about volts and ampères? What we want is justice!")

Until the First World War, nearly all civil cases were tried with juries, just as criminal cases were. But during that war the difficulty of getting sufficient numbers of jurymen—women were not yet eligible to sit as jurors—to staff the courts, without great dislocation of business, especially in London, led to more and more cases being tried without juries. Since it was found that trial by judge alone was better and quicker, and avoided the risk of juries disagreeing and the case having to be heard again, or of their being wrongly "directed" by the judge in his summing-up, with similar results, litigants turned more and more to non-jury trial, except in the class of cases, such as motor accident claims, where juries notoriously favoured plaintiffs. As there was little or no class element involved, the ruling class raised no objection. Litigants moved more and more to prefer non-jury trial, and we have now reached the position that civil cases cannot be tried with a jury unless an order is made to that effect, which is normally done only in cases of fraud or defamation.

Returning to the criminal law, I feel that the presence of the jury as a purely lay element in the trial of cases could create important dangers for the ruling class. The law is a weapon of the ruling class, and it has, as we have seen, taken care to make the whole weapon so reliable, and to keep it so securely in its own hands, that it is well protected against any results harmful to its interests by the composition of the apparatus of the law, including the judges. With the potential—and at some periods of history the actual—danger of juries acquitting citizens whom the ruling class particularly wants to suppress, I will deal in a moment.

I come now to consider how in practice trials with juries work out, for without that knowledge one cannot understand their relation to the class war. At first sight, in actual practice, one could hardly imagine a more unsuitable tribunal. Twelve persons, gathered together haphazard, strangers to one another, with no common bond except that they are all qualified to sit as jurors—I will discuss the important matter of their qualification a little lower down—and given no training or explanation to help them in their complicated duties beyond what they may glean from the judge's summing-up, which comes after they have heard all the evidence and the speeches of counsel. They sit in their "box" for a day or two and occasionally for weeks, longing perhaps to get to their work or their homes. They listen as best they can to the evidence—they are seldom shown more than one or two of the documents—and then do their best to reach a verdict.*

They suffer, inevitably, from a lack of all the disciplines and qualities which good judges possess in a high degree and all judges possess substantially: the realisation that they must do their best to clear their minds of anything they may have heard about the case outside the court; that they must sink their prejudices; must exclude from consideration any inadmissible evidence that may have been tendered or even (wrongly) admitted, and decide solely on what is properly admitted and proved in court; must eliminate anything that is less than proof and no more than suspicion (which involves the ability to know the boundary line between the two, something which takes lawyers years to master); must even ignore feelings of sympathy that may be based on poverty, wealth, race, politics, or anything else. The difficulties of such tasks for a jury are, I think, largely responsible for the existence of the tremendously complicated law of evidence, with which I will deal in Chapter 11.

With all these difficulties, how do juries do their work? Let me take criminal cases, the most important in volume and nature. Supporters of the system maintain that juries provide a real safeguard for accused persons, and acquit some who would be convicted by judges sitting alone. But most experienced lawyers hold that they not infrequently convict men whom the judges would feel bound to acquit. For very many years the view was complacently held, especially by the middle classes, with every encouragement from the establishment, that errors by

---

* In the prosecution of the late Lord Kylsant for fraud in 1931, in which I acted—it was not a very complicated case, and the jury came mostly from a business section of the population—one of the jurymen was overheard to say to another, as he came out of court at an adjournment: "I haven't the remotest idea what this case is all about, have you?" The other said that he had not, either.

juries, above all in murder cases, were quite impossible, for reasons which they were not able to state clearly. But gradually, by one instance after another, some in small cases and some in very grave ones, and some with virtual and some with absolute certainty, it has become clearly established that such errors can and do occur. (It is almost ironical to reflect that the only branch of our administration in which we have thus been reluctant to admit such a possibility is also the only branch in which errors are so well-known to happen that a whole apparatus of appellate courts is set up to correct the errors.)

The jury system works badly in other ways than by the conviction of innocent men. Not only do they cause, as I have mentioned, waste and expense by being unable to arrive at a verdict, but they seem pretty often to return verdicts, both by way of acquittal and conviction, which are perverse in the sense of being against the strong weight of the evidence, or—in the case of verdicts where they have to deal with several charges—inconsistent. One could quote many illustrations of this sort of bad working. A curious one, by no means extreme, was to be seen in the trial of the London and Liverpool dockers, mentioned above, where the verdict was so illogical that the prosecution had to drop the case. There was another example in the "Blaina Rioters" case, in which I appeared at the Monmouthshire Assizes during the long slump of the 'thirties which hit the mining industry with especial severity. The unemployed miners of Blaina—which at that time meant, of course, all the miners of Blaina—decided to hold a demonstration, which among Welsh miners and many others was a traditional and lawful method of voicing their grievances. The Chief Constable of the County was minded, for some reason, to see that they did not hold it, and presumed to "forbid" it, which he had no right to do. The miners were not prepared to swallow that, and decided to go ahead. The Chief Constable accordingly sent a mass of police, armed with batons, to prevent the demonstration being held. The police charged the demonstrators, and beat up a number of them. Then a dozen of them were prosecuted for riot. I need not relate the trial in detail, for it is only the way in which the jury—drawn incidentally, by a typical ruling-class trick, from the agricultural area of the county, where understanding and sympathy for the miners would not be so strong (I shall deal later in this Chapter with the right of citizens to be tried by their "peers")—gave their verdict that is interesting for our purposes. In addition to the general charge of riot against all the accused, there were separate charges against nearly all of them of assaulting the police, arising out of isolated incidents which took place when various miners were pursued by police after the demonstration had been broken up. Every policeman who gave evidence on the riot charge was also involved in one or other of the assault charges; and every one accused of assault was acquitted. This meant that all the police witnesses were disbelieved on their oath. And yet, on the evidence of these disbelieved witnesses, the accused were found guilty of riot.

Although, as I mentioned above, comparatively few civil cases are tried with juries, civil cases in their turn provide an unexpectedly large number of instances of curious behaviour by juries, perhaps because in these cases, especially fraud and defamation, at least one of the parties has enough money both to conduct the case with a high degree of elaboration and ingenuity and to take it to appeal. It is common to see civil verdicts which are plainly unreasonable, often in favour of plaintiffs who can afford to employ the so-called "fashionable" counsel, skilled in appealing to the prejudices of the jury, as a result of which a plaintiff who ought to lose in fact wins, or one who ought to recover £500 recovers £10,000. And the aggrieved defendant, if he can afford, must take the case to the Court of Appeal, where the question is not: "Which of these two litigants ought to win?", but: "Is this verdict so unreasonable that the Court must set it aside, or is there just enough evidence to compel the Court to say that the near-veneration which is paid to juries must allow the verdict to stand although they feel sure it is unreasonable?" As juries in civil cases are not essentially different from those in criminal cases, instances of this kind provide further ground for anxiety as to the reliability of verdicts in criminal cases.

If I may try to sum up, I think that, in respect of cases having no direct or indirect political flavour, and no element exciting indignation or prejudice, juries—judged by results—are not much worse, and certainly not much better, as judges of fact, than judges. But, so soon as politics come into the case,

F

especially when generally unpopular political views are involved, they present a major obstacle to progress.

Before coming to consider the dangers which the jury
system, with its introduction of a popular element into the
administration of justice, may present to the ruling class, I
must consider an aspect, and a possible justification of the
jury system, based on the desire, felt and expressed in many
countries, both capitalist and socialist, to secure that the
courts—at any rate at first instance, where the questions of
fact are largely decided—shall contain some non-professional
membership to counteract the legal element provided by the
professional judges, who may become hide-bound and technical
in their approach to cases, as well as remote from the mass of
the people and "establishment-minded". In many countries,
some popular control—even if a little remote—is achieved or
sought to be achieved by the system of electing judges by
direct popular vote. This works well in the socialist states, but
it has not been a success in the U.S.A. When I was in New York
some years ago, during an election of state judges, I saw an
advertisement on a hoarding: "Vote for judge —— and keep
the Commies out", which I read to mean that one of the
candidates was attempting to win or hold his office by accusing
one of his opponents of giving fair treatment to left-wing
accused. The British ruling class has always set its face sternly
against any such system, as I mentioned in Chapter 7, and in
any case it could not be nearly so valuable as the more direct
popular participation in the shape of laymen actually forming
part of the personnel of the courts. In most socialist countries,
the courts of first instance, and occasionally other courts, have
three members, one being an elected professional judge and the
other two laymen, drawn from panels of elected citizens and
sitting for a few weeks in each year. The professional judge is
the chairman, but if the three are not unanimous the decision
is by a majority, so that the two laymen can overrule the
professional judge on a point of law as well as on a point of
fact—of course, after a full discussion between the three, who
have to prepare jointly a written judgment. In capitalist
countries, there are two main methods of seeking some popular
participation. One—not in use in England—is that of lay
assessors, generally from two to five in number, either sitting

with the professional judge or separately, as the jury does in England. In the latter case, the judge at the end of the hearing— sometimes after summing up the case to them—asks for their opinion as to whether the accused is guilty or not. In some jurisdictions, their opinions are binding on the judge, and in others he is entitled to ignore them. (The assessor system was, and to some extent still is, widely used in India and in other former colonies of Britain. I shall deal with it in a later volume.)

The other system is that of the jury, with which I have already dealt. Here, too, there are varieties. For example, in West Germany the jury sit with the (three or so) professional judges as part of the court, and they all retire together to consider their decision, so that the judges have more opportunity to influence the jury. In most countries that use juries, however, the English system of having the jury sitting separately is followed.

I can now come to my main problem, more directly involving the class struggle, namely: how does the ruling class, always conscious of what it wants for the protection of its interests and determined to secure it, so manage the jury system that it can be confident of securing the verdicts it wants in cases important to the maintenance of its class strength? It cannot, of course, abolish the jury system. That would be much too crude for its subtlety, and would excite too much popular opposition, for it has adroitly persuaded much of the public to regard the jury as the "palladium of British justice", guaranteeing that "no man shall be convicted of a crime save by the verdict of his peers" ("peers", here, has its old meaning of "equals"). This is praised, with or without historical accuracy, as being derived from Magna Carta, the treaty of concessions extracted in 1215 by the English nobles from the then King John, and vaunted—again, with not too much historical accuracy—as the basis of the "liberty of the subject" in England. It laid down that:

"no freeman shall be taken or imprisoned or be dispossessed of his freehold land or liberties or free customs, or be outlawed or exiled or in any way destroyed; *nor will we pass upon him, nor condemn him, save by the lawful judgment of his peers, or by the law of the land*".

As there is no question of abolition, how did and does the

ruling class deal with the possible dangers of the jury system? There were and are in substance two methods. I will describe the less important and less complete one first. It consists of with-holding jury trial by the creation and application of innumer-able minor offences triable by magistrates sitting without juries. By this means, all but the gravest political "crimes" can be adequately punished without any jury having the opportunity to acquit. This manœuvre is to some small extent hampered by a provision that any person accused of a minor offence punishable by more than three months' imprisonment may demand, when he is charged in the magistrates' court, that the case shall not be tried there but be committed to the Assizes or Quarter Sessions, where he will be tried before a jury. The demand must be made at the beginning of the hearing. Not much use is made of this provision at present in political cases, since—as we shall see—the jury would be no more favour-able in such cases than the magistrates. It is used mostly by people who think that their particular case—or the class of cases into which it falls—is more likely to lead to conviction by the magistrates than by a jury. Motorists accused of danger-ous driving are the most frequent users at present, since most juries are car-drivers whilst magistrates hear so many such cases that they are more conscious of the dangers of bad driving.

The second of the two methods of "keeping the jury safe" is typically ingenious. It is to maintain the qualification for jury service at such a level that a jury seldom has more than one or two workers on it—generally, indeed, none at all—and is thus virtually certain to approach the decision of every important case with the outlook—say, the prejudices—of the ruling class, especially when there is any political or trade union element in it. It would be a very simple matter of legislation, if we have a Parliament that genuinely represented the working class, to broaden the qualifications, and thus wholly to destroy this particular safeguard. (The Labour government of 1945–50 did pass a "Juries Act, 1949" (12 and 13 Geo. 6, Chapter 27) to provide for payment to jurors and to abolish "special juries", which could until then be summoned by either party in civil actions at a small expense, and provided a somewhat more reactionary outlook, and it would have been very easy to take the opportunity to alter the jury qualifications in the sense I have suggested. It is perhaps significant of the development of the Labour leadership that this was not done.)

The present qualifications for jury service are, broadly, that all *residents* beneficially possessed of real estate or rent charges of the value of £10 per year (or of leaseholds for not less than 21 years of the value of £10 per year), or—and this is the general qualification—householders residing in premises of a net annual value of not less than £30 in London, or of £20 elsewhere, are liable to jury service if they are between 21 and 60 years old and do not fall in any exempted class such as lawyers, officers, and various officials (and various people with criminal convictions). One might not think that this qualification was very narrow, but if one takes the ordinary electors' roll in a working-class district, and looks for the letter J in the margin, which denotes liability for jury service, one sees how few people are actually qualified. The jurors thus qualified are treated as the "peers" of every person who comes to trial, whatever his origin, class or occupation. The right to be tried by one's peers has never been taken to mean that a worker should be tried by a worker, or a doctor by doctors (although for centuries it meant that a peer of the realm, if charged with felony, had to be tried by his peers in the House of Lords, and the elder brother of the late Bertrand Russell was so tried). There is only one list of jurors, to act as the peers of all of us. I can recall only one case* in over half a century of practice where there were more than one or two workers on a jury (and that in a country which has a higher proportion of its population in the working class than any other).

Workers are thus, in practice, tried not by their peers but by peers of the middle class. The phrase which I quoted above from Magna Carta—"save by the lawful judgment of his peers" should be recast, if it is to apply correctly, in modern English legislative language as: "lawful judgment of twelve citizens deemed in law to be his peers". (Indeed, to bring

---

* That was a political case in which a jury acquitted of sedition (a complicated common law offence which I will describe in a later volume; it has two disadvantages for the modern ruling-class prosecutor, the first that it has to be tried by a jury, and the second that for some reason juries nearly always acquit the accused) a Communist who had made a strong attack on the government. The rather unexpected acquittal brought an angry outburst from the judge, an able reactionary who had done all he could to persuade the jury to convict.

Magna Carta up to date from the point of view also of the manœuvres of trial by magistrates, one should add further: "or, where by the law of the land our justices of the peace may condemn without the presence of his peers".)

That is a complete description of the present apparently secure ruling-class position. But our alert rulers are no doubt continuously working to ensure by the manipulation of public opinion (and by shrewdly tailoring their own demands and actions so that they will not shock the manipulated public opinion) that they seldom find themselves confronted by a jury— which, if it happened at all, would probably mean by one jury after another—composed of citizens basically hostile to them and enjoying the advantage of not having to give—indeed of not having the right or opportunity to give—reasons for their verdicts, and ready to acquit, particularly in political cases, accused who are plainly guilty of the offence charged. Such difficulties are of the sort which the wily ruling class is and has generally been— alas!—highly skilled in combating, but it has seldom been seriously confronted with this particular difficulty since the days of Erskine in the latter part of the eighteenth century. At that time the reactionary ruling class, and the active and ambitious King George III with whom it was co-operating, were extremely frightened by the successful rebellion of the North American colonies and still more by the French Revolution, with its confiscation of landed property, and were at the same time confronted at home by an increasingly powerful mercantile community, and a militant proletariat born of the so-called industrial revolution. In the face of all these troubles, the ruling class, instead of just giving a little ground which it could recover later when the position was quieter, chose to fight hard like a frightened bully—after all, that is what it was—by introducing harsh legislation, especially against the workers, and bringing prosecutions under it. These prosecutions had to be tried before juries. The juries, drawn from the middle class which was hostile to the government, acquitted numbers of the accused whom the government was very eager to have sent to prison.

The ruling class tried one particular device at this period, in cases of alleged criminal libel, which was countered by an Act of Parliament (32 Geo. III, cap 60) called "Fox's Act", after Charles James Fox, who succeeded in getting it passed. I should explain this Act and the manœuvres which led up to it, for they are often misunderstood, and they have important political implications. The government lawyers, realising the danger of juries acquitting persons accused of libelling the government or the ministers, had managed to build up through the operation of case law the practice that it was for the judge and not for the jury to decide whether the words complained of did or did not constitute a libel. The result of this was that, if no more was proved than that the accused had in fact published the words complained of, the jury could be "directed", i.e., ordered, by the judge to find the accused guilty, although they wanted to acquit him because they did not object to the words said to be libellous. The matter came to a clash between judge and jury in the Dean of St. Asaph's case, reported in 4 Burrough's Reports, p. 73, where the jury, considering a satirical pamphlet attacking the King and approving it, wanted to acquit the accused, who had unquestionably written it. Confronted with the practice I have just stated, they brought in a verdict of "guilty of publishing only". The judge then harangued them for some time, and sent them back to think again, but they stuck as best they could to their guns, going only so far as: "guilty of publishing, but whether a libel or not the jury does not find".

This helped to bring the controversy to a head, and Parliament then passed Fox's Act, which recited that doubts had arisen as to whether on the general issue* a jury could give their verdict on the whole matter in issue, and went on to enact that:

> "on the trial of an indictment for a libel the jury may give a general verdict upon the whole matter put in issue, and shall not be required by the Court to find the defendant guilty merely on proof of the publication and of the sense ascribed to it in the Information".†

The present position, happy for the establishment, that juries are generally "safe" can only last as long as the social composition of juries and the general attitude of the strata of the

* "Verdict on the general issue" means in effect a verdict of "guilty" or "not guilty".

† Information was a procedure sometimes employed by the government to bring accused persons to trial direct. The "sense ascribed in the Information" thus means merely the sense alleged by the prosecution, which in the flowery language used by lawyers in those days would leave no doubt that it was libellous.

population from which they are drawn gives an adequate supply of jury members who are not only safe but are available to be taken from their ordinary occupations for periods in order to sit on juries without undue hardship. This position exists today in England, but in the colonial territories, including India and Ireland, with which I will deal in a later volume, it was very different. (In Ireland, during the "hungry forties" of the nineteenth century, for example, coroner's juries sitting on the bodies of men who had died of starvation invariably returned verdicts of "murder by the Chief Secretary for Ireland".)

It is useful to look at the position a little "inside out", as it were, that is to say, not to see how a jury might or may hamper the government in the conduct of the class war but to consider how today juries, as safe elements in the apparatus of class justice, may tend to convict those accused of political offences. I shall discuss this at length in a later volume, but I can say a little here about the effect of pro-establishment prejudice in the minds of most jurymen in civil cases for libel or slander. (Libel is written defamation, and slander is spoken defamation; and defamation, roughly, is anything which a jury thinks may bring the victim into hatred, contempt or ridicule.) Today, prosecutions for criminal libel are rare, but actions for libel are numerous, costly, and often, for good or ill, very important. The trouble here arises where progressive persons are attacked, especially in the "popular" newspapers. Every experienced barrister has to advise progressive clients who have been attacked in this way roughly to the following effect:

"This document is clearly libellous of you, and if you were a Tory so libelled by anyone on the Left you would have a strong case. But if you bring an action, the defendant will ask for a jury, and will get one, and the jury will soon be led to feel prejudiced against you because of your political views, which they do not share. The judge will probably tell them not to let prejudice affect their minds, but this will have little or no effect on them.

"The defendant will almost certainly raise the defence of 'fair comment', which means that he will win not only if his comment is really fair but also if it is one which—whether one agrees with it or not—a man might reasonably express and believe in. When the judge sums up, he will have to tell the jury that, if they think the comment fair in that sense, they must give a verdict for the defendant, which they will be delighted to do. Then you will have to pay your own costs and those of the other side too. This will go far to ruin you. I can only advise you not to sue."

In this way, the jury system renders substantial service—silently—to the class war by preventing progressives from complaining of unjust attacks on them, and by giving "the green light" to libellous reactionaries to write as harshly and inaccurately as they like about their Left-wing opponents.* And the damage works in reverse too, in that Left-wing writers wishing to criticise the establishmentarians have to be told by their lawyers that what *they* write is very likely to be made the subject of proceedings in which the prejudice will operate against them and that they will probably lose the case. The result, similarly, is that the Left Wing has to refrain from writing a good deal of honest criticism which ought to be written, but which carries the risk of heavy expenses in a libel action. (Moreover, if the writer feels so strongly that what he wants to write should be written that he decides to take the risk, he finds that his printer, even if friendly, will not print, for he would be as fully liable as the writer.)

* I had an interesting illustration—which fortunately I managed to frustrate—of the extent to which this can be carried, at the time when I was defending Jomo Kenyatta and five of his colleagues in Kenya against the charge of managing the illegal organisation "Mau Mau". Their defence was that they had no connection with Mau Mau. One day a prominent Right-wing daily paper in London, which to my knowledge managed its publication efficiently and—within its limits—honestly, printed in its correspondence "out of the blue" a letter from a "lady of title" in Kenya, in which she plainly implied that I was a supporter of Mau Mau, and was acting as an apologist for it in defending Kenyatta. The serious thing about this was that the case was still pending and that the defence was, as I have said, that there was no connection between Kenyatta and his colleagues and Mau Mau, so that such an assertion was prejudicial to the defence and was probably a contempt of court as well as a libel on me. I reacted immediately with a writ for libel and the newspaper had to make an apology in open court within a week, and in addition to publish a very handsome apology in its columns. The astonishing thing about the whole matter was that such a competent newspaper should have published the letter. It was plainly libellous, it was almost certainly a contempt of court, and the main point it made—that a lawyer who defends criminals is an accomplice in their crime—was so silly and politically illiterate that it should have ensured that the letter remained unprinted. I asked the solicitor whom I employed, an old-fashioned Liberal, how such a paper could print such a letter, and he answered without hesitation that the Press thought it could get away with anything if it was dealing with the Left Wing.

IO

Lawyers

THE legal profession in England, like so much of the apparatus of the law, is a complicated machine, and before I can discuss its effects and functions in the field of the class struggle I must give a short account of its present structure and organisation. I begin with an explanation of the meaning of the word "lawyer". To laymen, it means someone who practises law either as a barrister or a solicitor. To those who practise law, it often has the same meaning, though it is sometimes used by them to describe a solicitor as distinct from a barrister, but the word has for them also a different and less precise meaning, denoting one who is not merely a professionally qualified lawyer but actually has a really good knowledge of the law. Such a use may surprise laymen, who think that all qualified lawyers must know the law well and are not much good unless they do. In truth much of the work done by both barristers and solicitors, in court or out of it, can be done pretty well with no more than a basic knowledge of the law. What one calls "good lawyers" are invaluable only in certain fields, and for some cases.

The legal profession in England is, and for centuries has been, divided into two separate branches, barristers and solicitors, having largely different training and functions, and having indeed had, until less than half a century ago, differences in social status not unlike the old differences between apothecaries and surgeons. Nowadays, these differences have virtually disappeared, and it is becoming progressively easier for individuals to change over from one branch to the other.

Barristers are collectively called "the bar", deriving that name from the fact that they were qualified to come to the bar or barrier in the court and address the judge. They are often called "counsel", the plural of the word also being "counsel". Although barristers can and do do a certain amount of work in advising, their main work, at any rate in the common law field, including the criminal law, lies in the conduct of cases before the courts. They have the exclusive right of audience in the superior courts and at Assizes, and in most but not all Quarter Sessions. Solicitors are admitted to conduct cases in County Courts, Magistrates' Courts, and in Quarter Sessions in areas where barristers are not readily available.

There are about 2,000 barristers practising in England and Wales (less, it is said, than the number of solicitors practising in the little City of London alone). Perhaps as many as a quarter of them have their offices in the larger provincial towns, and the rest in London, where they congregate in the Temple, Lincoln's Inn, and less thickly in Grays Inn. From any modern point of view, barristers occupy an anomalous position. Their relations with solicitors and their lay clients—called "lay" to distinguish them from solicitors, who from the barrister's point of view are also clients—are not contractual, they are not entitled in law to their fees, and they cannot be sued for negligence. They practise as individuals, and cannot enter into partnership with one another. No lay client may approach or deal with, or even see, a barrister except through and in the company of his solicitor (or one of his clerks). When any layman is in need of legal advice or other assistance, he must begin by employing a solicitor, who will—either almost at once, or at a later stage, or perhaps not at all, according to the nature of the client's needs—take him to a barrister. This cumbrous and expensive procedure is of convenience to barristers, who are thus protected from being "button-holed" by lay clients, and are spared the laborious and patience-trying work of slowly extracting as accurate an account as possible of the facts of the matter from a layman who has not been trained to tell a story chronologically and whose narrative will often be warped by his natural prejudice in his own favour and sometimes by a reluctance to tell the whole truth about the difficult points. The system annoys lay clients not a little, and deprives barristers of first-hand contact with the practical problems and anxieties of the lay clients, since they learn practically everything "second-hand" from papers, after the solicitor has gathered it from the lay client, tidied it up, and had it typed out. It is probably true that this isolation of barristers—or, better, the whole elaborate "double-decker" organisation of the profession, of which it is a part—leads through the resulting specialisation, to higher skill and efficiency in the conduct of cases (to which both barrister and solicitor make important contributions); but the price of this advantage in terms of expense and cumbrous operation is very high.

Solicitors, formerly called "attorneys" in the common law courts and "solicitors" in the Chancery courts, are now always called "solicitors". There are over 22,000 practising in England and Wales, and even then their services are in such demand that a few thousand more are really needed. Their function is to give their clients all the legal advice and service which barristers do not render, including the preparation of cases for barristers to give advice or to conduct the case in court, and including too—for those solicitors who care to undertake it—the conduct of cases in courts where they have a right to appear. They can, and generally do, enter into partnership with other solicitors, and they can employ other solicitors, as well as unqualified clerks, to work in their practices. Their relations with their clients are a matter of contract, and subject to certain limitations they may make arrangements with their clients as to their remuneration, may sue for it, and are liable for negligence (there are so many ways in which, in matters of routine as well as in matters calling for professional skill, a solicitor or his clerks may trip up that it is normal to take out insurance against such risks).

The remuneration of barristers is arranged by the solicitor on behalf of the lay client with the barrister's clerk. Although, as I have said, the barrister cannot sue for his fees, the solicitor is as a matter of professional duty bound to pay them, and must therefore protect himself against any failure of the lay client, which he commonly does by insisting on being put in the necessary funds before he goes to the barrister.

Lawyers, although—or because?—they are just as strongly entrenched in the machinery of government and indeed in the life of the country as the judges and magistrates, have through the centuries been hated by the "lower orders" in England, as in many other countries. This is not, in my view, mainly or even largely due to their wealth or superior education, nor even to the opportunities—of which from time to time some of them take advantage—provided by their skill in the law to exploit their clients. It is rather that the mass of the people, who are apt to see through to the essence of any situation, even if they are not always able to state their views clearly, realise very well, and resent, the way the minority ruling class exploits and oppresses them, and logically extend their resentment to the agents of the ruling class, among whom they rightly number the lawyers, as they do the police.

Let me see what are the real demerits—and merits too—of the lawyers. It is clear that they are not only an essential part of the law as ruling-class machinery, but are also as necessary to the ordinary citizen when he finds himself in contact with the law as are, say, doctors when he is ill. But we must look further than that.

I may start by examining how well, or how badly, lawyers—especially barristers, but solicitors have their place too—behave when called upon to act for clients whose views or actions, rightly or wrongly, excite public indignation. Such cases include, but range rather wider than, the political matters of which I have already written a good deal, and in a later volume I shall deal more extensively with the problems of political prosecutions. I have dealt in Chapters 7, 8 and 9 with reactions of judges, magistrates and juries on such points, and lawyers are almost as essential a part of the machinery calling for consideration here as are the three mentioned. So, how do the lawyers behave? I will deal first with barristers, whose attitudes and problems I know more fully. The position of solicitors is not basically different, even if they may be confronted less often and less acutely than barristers by the difficulties I have to discuss.

Barristers seldom specialise from the start of their careers. They normally begin by waiting for cases. They may or may not have long to wait, but they are sure to have too few cases at first to take up all their time, and certainly far too few to enable them to pick and choose. They will be glad of anything that comes. If—as will happen if some of their early work is in criminal cases—some of their clients seem to be rascals and very likely guilty of the crimes charged against them, the barristers will soon learn that such characters have as much right as anyone else to legal representation, and are in more need of it than most. They will take these cases with a clear conscience. But after a time they get more work. Nearly all of them, although they are able to pick and choose, will tend to follow the conventional line that they are there to conduct all cases that come their way, whether they like their lay clients' views and activities or not, and will feel that they are not identifying themselves in any way with the clients, but merely presenting their cases as well as they can. (As one well-known and respected criminal advocate put it: "I defend burglars all day long, but no one suggests that I have to be a burglar myself to defend them, or even that I approve of burglary.") The nearest a barrister is likely to get to picking and choosing in his early days will probably come when he is offered two or more cases at the same time, and can only take one of them. Then he will probably take the case that pays best, or one which comes from a busy solicitor whom he hopes to make into a regular client, or one whose work lies in a field of practice, e.g., civil rather than criminal, contract rather than tort, or whatever it may be, in which the young man would prefer in the long run to develop his practice. That is "all right so far", but in the end the man may find himself invited to take a case which does not commend itself to his political or social prejudices and beliefs, or even to his conscience, and he may feel incapable of conducting it forcefully, with a detached mind, as he could if his client were merely a burglar. What is he to do then? It is worth our while to consider his difficulties at length, for they lie at the root of the whole problem of political defences, i.e., of the important matter of securing adequate and understanding legal representation for citizens whose views are at the moment abhorrent to the majority, although they may be recognised as socially valuable in a few years' time.

What is he to do? If he is prudent, he will seek the advice of an older and more experienced colleague (and it is one of the virtues of a profession in which I worked happily, if stormily, for half a century, that we all feel ourselves entitled to ask, and bound to give one another honest advice in such problems). From this advice, he will learn that it is in theory a rule of the profession that barristers are bound to conduct any case which falls within the general scope of their practice, regardless of their personal attitude to their client's views. He may be re-

minded that in the eighteenth and nineteenth centuries many
political accused were well defended by some of the finest
advocates of the time, and that the system did not work too
badly. Barristers of upper- or middle-class outlook seemed
then to be able at least to understand the motives that had
actuated many people accused of riot, or sedition, or treason,
sufficiently to defend them well, not "pulling their punches"
out of fear of the government or of distaste for their clients.
He will also learn that, if he wants to escape from the duty
to take a case which he is in theory bound to take, there are
half a dozen perfectly good plausible excuses that he can advance
for doing so. If his adviser knows as much about the conduct of
political cases as I think that I do, he will probably add that in
the last fifty years or so the gulf in ideas between those—
Communist or Left-wing Labour, or even at times pacifist—
who are likely to find themselves in the dock for their political
activities on the one hand, and members of the class from which
barristers are still largely drawn on the other, has become so
deep that it is now almost impossible for the average barrister
even to understand the essence of such cases sufficiently well to
defend them adequately. Indeed, that by reason of this gulf
most potential accused will have no confidence that they can
be adequately defended except by counsel pretty near to their
own views. And so, in the end, these accused have to be
defended by barristers and solicitors of their own point of view.
And even today, when the social origins of lawyers are far less
exclusively upper or middle class than they were, they are only
barely enough barristers with sufficient understanding and
sympathy to do the work. (For, alas!, part of the cunning of
the ruling class is spent on securing that most of the people of
lower middle-class or working-class origin who make their
way into the legal profession begin to take on the colour of
the majority of their colleagues, and are thus "lost". The position
with solicitors is not basically different, although probably less
acute.)

I feel bound to conclude that, although there are at any
moment just enough Left-wing lawyers available to supply fairly
well the needs of Left-wing clients, the profession does on the
whole fail to provide adequate service in this field. It may be
that, in the existing political atmosphere and in the light of the

education and social background of nearly all barristers and very many solicitors, such failure is inevitable, but it is a fact with which we must reckon. The temptation to keep away from such cases, or to "pull punches", must always be present, and its very possibility tends to make clients suspect its presence when it may not be there.*

The gaps, and the dangers of minority opinions being inadequately protected, remain. I recall with horror a case which I followed during the First World War. A young barrister whom I knew fairly well was a conscientious objector, and he had a case in the High Court which showed reasonable prospect of securing him either release from prison or more humane treatment whilst there. His father, a rich man who had no sympathy with his views but was ready to help him, engaged a leading barrister at considerable expense to appear for him. This barrister, a bitter reactionary and a loud-mouthed "patriot" who managed to reconcile his enthusiasm for the war with continuing to carry on his profitable practice all the time, had so little feeling for his duties to his client that he took up much of his time in the conduct of the case in explaining to the court what it already knew, namely—that he had no sympathy with his client's views. The result of this strange and inadequate method of "fighting" was that he lost the case. The barrister collected his fee, and went on to become Lord Chancellor. The client committed suicide.

What some barristers lack for this difficult branch of their work is courage. It needs courage to get up in court and present a very unpopular standpoint, and the courage, or high sense of duty, needed is not lessened by the consideration that, in this not very clear thinking world, the barrister is almost certain to lose clients by doing so. I had a curious illustration towards the end of my practising years of the extent to which some

---

* I have at times been asked, especially by foreigners, to find them first-class legal advisers for individuals or for foreign governments, and have replied:

"I cannot find you an experienced adviser who is also politically sympathetic, for the sympathetic have not yet had the opportunity to develop the experience and the high technical skill necessary for such matters as yours. But I can—repeat can—find you in this curious country competent legal advisers, not sympathetic to your point of view, who will nevertheless have the courage and integrity to give you sincere and unbiased service. You may find this very difficult to believe; but I can assure that I am right."

On not a few occasions, my advice was accepted, and proved to be right.

barristers will run away from their duties for fear of losing clients. A solicitor whom I did not know, practising in a part of the country with which I had no connection, brought me a case of a kind rather outside the normal run of my practice. It involved a charge of neglect of duty—not of any malpractice— against a well-known and very busy London solicitor. There seemed to be no reason why I should not take the case, for a reasonable fee. I took the fee, conducted the case, and won it, in my view rightly. When it was all over, I asked the solicitor why he had brought the case to me, and he answered: "Well, we offered it to a dozen barristers, all of whom would be the natural people to conduct such a case, and they all began with one accord to make excuse. We are quite sure—indeed, we learnt expressly from some of them—that their motive in refusing was that they did not want to take a case of that nature against that solicitor, for they were afraid of not getting any work from him if they did."*

Problems of this sort apart, there is much to be written about the merits and defects of lawyers, and it is the more necessary to write about them because much of the criticism levelled against lawyers is, to my mind, with such impartiality as I can command, not justified.

One merit, which I have found almost universal among barristers—and I have no reason to suppose that solicitors are any different—is that they are nearly all honest in the sense that they cheat neither the court nor their clients, and are fair in their dealings with one another. It is almost unknown for a barrister to try to "steal" a case or a client away from another, or even to tout or advertise (most barristers could name exceptions, including a few well-known names, but only one or two).

Turning to defects, let me begin with those that really do exist. One of the worst, not widespread, but far too common, is the practice of encouraging clients to carry on cases that have no real chance of success. It is tempting. For if a barrister or a solicitor gives a client's case serious thought and then advises him not to sue, he will earn perhaps only one-hundredth of what he would get if the client was persuaded to carry the case

---

* It is true that the solicitor who was sued in the case, who knew me well and occasionally sent me work, would not speak to me for some years after the case. But we became good friends in the end.

G

to trial. That this defect is not universal is shown by the fact that the great majority of both branches of the profession will always tell their clients that it is better to settle any dispute on reasonable terms than to carry it through to trial.

Another defect, more frequent than it should be, for ideally it should never be seen at all, is that cases are often not fully or adequately investigated and prepared by solicitors, or not fully mastered by barristers. This, when it happens, is due partly to pressure of work, partly to the fact that some of the personnel involved are not sufficiently trained for their often very difficult work, and at times of course to sheer carelessness or indifference.

Then I come to alleged defects that are generally, but not of course always, non-existent. The most usual complaint, and perhaps the least justified, is the assertion that the solicitor— or occasionally the barrister—is "in league with the other side", to which is often added the assertion that "he forced me to settle the case instead of fighting it and winning". In my fifteen years as a London M.P., when my constituents came to me at the rate of over a hundred a week with every imaginable problem, quite a few of them concerning cases in which they were involved, these assertions were the most common, arising in perhaps half the litigation brought to my notice. These complaints—mostly unjustified—arose partly from an ingrained suspicion of lawyers, partly because solicitors—whilst really doing their best for their clients—were often too busy to sit down and give them full explanations of what they had thought right to do, and partly, naturally, because clients, looking at the case from their own point of view, and not seeing the difficulties, just cannot understand why greater success has not been achieved. Solicitors and barristers can more easily see the difficulties of a case, and understand how much better it would be to accept some kind of settlement, which only achieves perhaps half of what the client thinks he ought to have (and perhaps twice what the client on the other side thinks he ought to be made to pay) than to risk going on to the bitter end.

There is often a somewhat similar complaint, that the lawyers did not call a witness that the client thinks they should have called. This can at times be right, but is much more often un-justified. Litigation is very complicated, and a client who thinks that a particular witness ought to have been called is rather like a patient who wants to tell the doctor how he ought to treat him. The lawyer will often know that what the suggested witness would say would be inadmissible under the rules of evidence, or that it would actually be harmful to the case, or that under cross-examination the witness would have to admit facts which the other side had not yet managed to prove, and which, again, might be harmful to the client's case. And their decision not to call the witness may be absolutely correct. The client may well not understand this until it is fully explained to him, and there is often no opportunity to give him the explanation until after the decision, which can sometimes be taken only in court, on a view of the position just about the time when the witness would be called. Explanations to a disappointed client after the case is over do not come at a time when he is particularly receptive.

At the end of the story of defects, I come to one which is not really a defect of the lawyers but rather of the whole of the "free world" system under which we still have to work. I have in mind the position of lawyers who conduct cases for rich clients, who naturally seek—as I mentioned above—to win cases by running up the expense of litigation until their opponents, having a shorter purse, are starved into submission. The richer side's lawyers, without seeing anything wrong, and indeed in fulfilment of their duty to their client, will put forward and argue this or that interlocutory application to the court, or some other proceeding, so long at any rate as they can be regarded as helpful to the presentation of their client's case. I shall write more about this matter in the next Chapter.

Now, let me consider the virtues or merits, some of which I have mentioned already. In part they are the reverse of the picture I have given on the defects. Most barristers and solicitors, as I have said, are honest; most have a high conception of the high duties they owe to their clients; and most have a fair measure of courage, even if not enough for some purposes. It must be remembered that the qualities demanded of lawyers are many and difficult to acquire. I am not referring to the educational qualifications demanded, which are fairly onerous, but to the various character-qualities which in the long run make good lawyers. For a barrister, they do not primarily or essentially include a profound knowledge of the law, but they include a capacity to think quickly and yet soberly whilst on one's feet, and an ability to read the mind of the judge or a jury to see what is impressing them one way or another. There are many other qualities too, such as tact, patience, and good manners. (I remember once, when I had been invited to address a private meeting to talk over the qualities of my profession, and mentioned in my speech these three qualities, I felt it necessary to add that I still did not understand how any solicitor had ever sent me more than one case.)

The qualities required of solicitors are similar, with the important and onerous addition that, as they are dealing directly all day long with lay clients, they must be able to adjust the speed of their thought and their method of expression to the slower and less widely informed, but not by any means necessarily less intelligent, processes of thought and expression of most of their clients.

As part of the merits and defects, one must reckon, for barristers and advocate-solicitors, the skill of rightly choosing both the manner and the content of the speeches on questions of fact they must present to the judge or jury before whom they are appearing. I say "questions of fact", for I think that on questions of law the arguments are really exercises of logical reasoning between judges and advocates who are on equal terms and have the same materials to deal with, so that their tasks are far easier, *if* they are good lawyers and have done their research properly. There are, I think, only two problems. The first is that, when addressing a less knowledgeable court, one must put the argument more slowly and more simply, especially in the case of magistrates, of whom I wrote something in Chapter 8; and the second, more difficult, concerns how far one is justified in putting to a judge a proposition of law which one "knows" to be bad ("knowing", here, can mean no more than that, as a lawyer, one is convinced that it is bad). The difficulty is that law is so uncertain, and the quality of judges so varied, that the argument which one "knows" to be wrong may appeal to the judge, and indeed that it may not be wrong at all! Probably one is justified in putting forward any argument of this sort, so long as one bears in mind the risk that, if the case is taken to appeal, and one meets with better judges there, one may lose the point, and suffer for ever having taken it. An able Australian barrister who appeared with me in cases before the Privy Council years ago (and later became Chief Justice of Australia) put the matter very simply and firmly: "No argument of law is too bad to put if the judge before whom you are appearing will accept it."

Coming back to the question of speeches on questions of fact, I think that the selection of both manner and content is a simple matter of human judgment as to how one can best impress this judge or this jury with the strength of one's case. How far-seeing are they? What will appeal to them, and what will not? Is it a case for kid gloves, or is the right way to bring the court round to attack a litigant who is open to attack? One may do a lot of harm by wrong tactics in this respect. I remember a case (Greenlands v. Wilmshurst, (1913) 2 K.B. 507; see at p. 52) in which the then Mr. F. E. Smith, afterwards Lord Birkenhead, an able but flamboyant and reckless advocate, appearing for the defendants in a libel action, had made a strong attack in his final speech against a plaintiff whom the jury liked. The jury gave the plaintiff heavy damages, and the defendants appealed to the Court of Appeal, asking for a new trial on the question of damages. The Court of Appeal ordered this, and in the course of his judgment one of the judges, the then Lord Justice Hamilton, who soon afterwards became a Lord of Appeal under the title of Lord Sumner, an extremely able judge, a great master of the common law, and an extremely sarcastic person before whom it was not easy to argue, dealt with the matter thus;

> "It is said that an imputation on a trader's credit is grave, and I agree; that the jury may express their sympathy with the plaintiff at the defendant's expense and mark their sense of the defendant's misconduct in the same way. . . . It is said that the defendant's counsel set the jury against him by the impetuosity of his attack on the plaintiff, and that the jury could inflame the damages for that. Still, in my opinion, by no formula or manipulation can £1,000 [the sum awarded by the jury] be got at. For any damage really done, £100 was quite enough: double it for the sympathy: double it again for the jury's sense of the defendants'

conduct, and again for their sense of Mr. F. E. Smith's. The product is only £800."

One of the hardships of the barrister's life in court is that, whilst the judges, as I mentioned in Chapter 7, may treat them with great discourtesy, they have to be almost exaggeratedly respectful to the judges. They must not say: "You are wrong", or even: "Your Lordship is wrong." Scarcely even is it permissible to say: "Surely your Lordship is wrong." One has to say something like: "I humbly submit that your Lordship has not stated it quite accurately." Far worse, and more frustrating, is the rule that counsel must never interrupt the judge, however mistaken he may be, and that the judge may always interrupt counsel, as often as he chooses and at any moment, however inconvenient to the statement of an argument. With good judges, who time their interruptions considerately, and make helpful ones, the system works well with good counsel, who can keep their memories and know what they want to say, because it helps to get to the real point of the case; but it calls for high skill from counsel. In the Privy Council, I invented and often used a formula: "My next argument cannot well be formulated in less than three uninterrupted sentences." This usually secured a smile, and the opportunity to get out two uninterrupted sentences.

I I

The Law in Operation in the Courts

SOME knowledge of the way in which cases are actually conducted in court, whether civil or criminal, and whether the
State is a party to the case or not—as it is to every criminal
case and quite a few civil ones—is necessary for all who seek to
understand both the general function of the law as a ruling-
class weapon and the inequalities of litigation as between
rich and poor litigants—this latter being a result rather of the
advantages reaped by members of the more powerful class
against the rest than of any *direct* operation of the class struggle.

The whole operation of carrying cases through the courts is
called by lawyers "procedure"; and the law of evidence
comes so closely into the picture that one can treat it here with
procedure. The same may be said as to the law relating to the
interpretation of documents, called by lawyers "construction"
(from the word "construe", not from "construct"). Interpretation is a more important part of the apparatus of the law—
and in some respects more of a weapon in the class struggle—
than one might think.

I will start with procedure in the narrower sense—how cases
are presented to and decided by the courts. Laymen might
think that this would be pretty simple; if two citizens are
in dispute, let them go to the court and put the matter before a
judge, or, if the state accuses someone of a crime, let it take him
to court and thrash out the question of his guilt or innocence.
But life is never so simple as that. In order both to deal fairly
with any legal conflict and to avoid endless confusion in
court, a number of preliminary steps, called "interlocutory",
have to be taken before a case comes before a judge. The issues
to be tried must be clearly defined, so that both sides may know
what they must deal with in preparing to prove their side of the
case, and to rebut the other side's case, when they get into

court. And, as I have mentioned, the necessary cost of these generally necessary "interlocutory" proceedings can be greatly increased by rich litigants so as to make the case impossible for the other side. To illustrate the great elaboration to which this preparatory work has been carried, I may say that, when I was called to the Bar over sixty years ago, there were published *annually* two competing text-books on procedure in the Supreme Court, each containing over 4,000 pages of small print, dealing with a large volume of procedural legislation entitled "The Rules of the Supreme Court", and citing many thousands of reported decisions on procedure. Today, these two publications have been merged into one, still published annually, the 1970 issue of which has 6,527 pages and cites about 9,000 cases, dealing largely with the 112 "Orders of the Supreme Court" comprised within the "Rules of the Supreme Court".

I will deal first with civil cases in the Supreme Court, then with civil cases in the County courts, and then with criminal cases. To define the issues in a case in the High Court of Justice—the section of the Supreme Court in which cases are tried at first instance—after the plaintiff has brought the case into being by issuing a writ, the issues are defined by formal and carefully drafted documents called "pleadings" (the word, like many lawyers' words, is misleading to laymen, who think of pleadings as oral arguments in court) prepared by the barristers of the two parties and exchanged between them, in which the plaintiff sets out shortly the essential facts he hopes to prove and the relief he claims against the defendant, and the latter in his pleading gives his answer to the claim (and may perhaps put forward a "counterclaim"—for once, a word that the layman can understand). This does not sound too complicated, but in practice the preparation of these pleadings, and of "further particulars" of the allegations made in them, takes up a good many weeks, and involves a substantial sum in fees to the barristers and solicitors. And, of course, in order to put the case of each side at its best in the pleadings, a good deal of preliminary work of investigating and gathering of evidence must be done at this early stage (not all of which will be wasted when the general preparation begins, after the issues have been defined). These issues, as I have said, are defined by the pleadings, and when these have been "closed" (i.e., finished) because each party has put forward all he wants to say at this stage, the work of preparation goes forward. It is made more difficult by the rules of evidence, which I shall discuss later, with their elaborate and technical provisions as to what material may be used to prove anything, and what may not. The work of preparation is not all done "at home", by each side in the absence of the other; for the procedure includes a valuable—but of course expensive—system, historically derived from the Chancery courts, and helpful to both sides and to the tidy, speedy and just disposal of the case. It is called "discovery of documents" (discovery here means disclosure). Each side has to state on affidavit what documents material to the case are or have been in its possession, and must then show them to the other side and let it have copies of them. This system greatly helps the preparation and conduct of the case, saves the parties from surprise, and may indeed so clarify a case that one party or the other may realise that it has a weak case and had better try to arrange a settlement (as lawyers call a compromise). But, of course, it adds once more to the cost of litigation, and gives to the richer litigant one more legitimate opportunity to make the case so costly for the poorer opponent that the latter, honestly advised by his solicitor, may perhaps never embark on a case at all, or may, when he has started, be driven by the unbearable expense to drop it, or make a settlement on unfavourable terms. This makes procedure not exactly into a weapon of the class war but at the least a weapon of the rich litigant, generally belonging to the one class, against his poorer opponent, often belonging to the other. All this involves injustice, often with an element of vicious circle about it, since the weapon will not only be used when a case arises, but cases of no merit will be launched in the knowledge that the defendant cannot "stay the course" and will have to pay something, and defences of no merit will be put forward against genuine claims by poorer men, who will be starved into dropping or settling the case.*

* The trick can be used the other way round, against richer people. Poor men, speculatively financed by others, may launch actions which the rich defendant may be glad to settle for perhaps £50, knowing that it will cost him more than £50 to fight and win the case, and that the plaintiff will not be able to pay. In the early days of motoring, a famous car-manufacturer decided as a matter of policy that he would never contest a case in court, but would rather settle on inadequate terms, thinking that any case would bring publicity that would "hurt

This particular evil has been reduced in recent years by the system of legal aid. I need not go into detail, but I can give the essence of it by saying that any litigant, whether plaintiff or defendant, who is unable to meet the heavy expenses of litigation can obtain the services of solicitor and counsel wholly or partly at the public expense, if he can obtain a certificate from a semi-official body showing that he has a reasonable case and cannot himself meet the cost. The quality of service thus provided is little inferior to that which the rich litigant can buy for himself, and the grant of certificates is not made too grudgingly. Perhaps the weakest part of the system comes, unfortunately, right at the beginning, in the stage of getting advice before any litigation has begun. This aid is, perhaps, only "tinkering", but it is good tinkering.

Coming back to the progress of a case in the High Court: when it is finally prepared, and ready to go into court for the hearing, the solicitor and the "junior" counsel having already done a good deal of work—"junior" counsel does not mean young counsel, but counsel of any age who have not become "Queen's Counsel"—a Q.C., as Queen's Counsel are often called, is generally brought in to take on the main burden of the conduct of the case, the lay client thus finding that he has to employ and pay three highly skilled lawyers.*

The employment of Q.C.s requires some explanation, and perhaps justification. It is of course one more addition to the expense, and one more advantage to the longer purse, of the sort I have already described, but it has its justification from the point of view of the efficient conduct of litigation. The conduct of cases in this country, with its many complications, including the laws of evidence, is extremely difficult and calls for high skill and indeed specialisation. A certain number of barristers, after some years, if they have built up a good practice and a good reputation, will apply to the Lord Chancellor to

his image". This policy decision leaked out to one or two unscrupulous people, and the manufacturer was soon swamped with pretty baseless claims, and had to change his policy. (But the general balance of this "wealth v. poverty" operation is, of course, heavily the other way.)

* In difficult cases, the advice of a Q.C. is sometimes taken at a much earlier stage, occasionally even before a writ is issued. In a very important and indeed famous case, Liversidge v. Anderson, with which I shall deal in a later volume, the Q.C., myself, was called in to design, as it were, the way in which the case should be presented, before the writ was issued, in order to prevent the government "sliding out" on a technicality.

appoint them to be Q.C.s—so far as giving counsel to the Queen is concerned, the title is a sinecure—in order that they may specialise in the conduct of cases of a fair size and complexity. As etiquette bars them from doing much of the work that is done by "junior" barristers, and from appearing in a case without a junior, they are as it were driven into this sort of specialisation. The result is—and herein lies the substantial justification of the system—that a case is somewhat better conducted by Q.C.s than by the general run of juniors. It is true that a good many juniors can conduct cases very well—after all, they will be joining the ranks of the Q.C.s in a few years—and the practice is growing of employing experienced juniors without Q.C.s to "lead" them in court. Solicitors will often agree with the other side that neither of them will employ a Q.C. in a particular case. But the practice of employing Q.C.s still persists, for several reasons. To begin with, it is unhappily true that judges, however hard they try not to do so, in fact pay more attention to what Q.C.s say than they do to juniors, unless the latter happen to be as good as Q.C. What judges want, especially in the early stage of a case, is a clear and understandable narrative of the facts, and a clear statements of any arguments of law— and, if possible, no long argument on clearly bad points. They have no previous knowledge of a case, beyond the bare bones of it which they can get from the pleadings, and are correspondingly pleased to be quickly enlightened.

That is a perfectly good and honest reason for the employment of this additional barrister, as is the next reason that, by the time any substantial case is ready for hearing, both the solicitor and the junior counsel have seen so much of it that they are a bit "stale", and the introduction at that stage of a fresh mind, who can look at the whole picture without the burden of having been engaged for months in constructing it, can be of substantial benefit because the Q.C. sees gaps that need to be filled up, and even new ways of putting the case that may call for amendment of the pleadings. I have seen a good many cases, competently prepared, that have eventually been won only because the Q.C., coming in at the last moment, has seen some defect and been able to cure it before it is too late.

The last of the main reasons for the employment of Q.C.s is much less praiseworthy, although cogent enough. It is that the practice has long been established that neither the Q.C. nor the junior is expected to attend in court throughout the whole of the hearing of a case unless he has specially agreed to do so (for a higher fee!). If they are good at their work, they probably have at any particular moment two or three cases being actually heard, and run from one to the other as they are needed, leaving a colleague to attend to the one they are quitting for the moment. This practice must seem to laymen utterly indefensible but it is well established, and the only defence for it—if one can call it a defence—is that the moment, or the hour, or even the day, at which a case which is in the list for hearing will actually come on is so unpredictable that if barristers, whether Q.C.s or juniors, never accepted a case unless they were sure of being able to attend throughout, they would very seldom accept a case at all. (There is a story from my early days of a very popular Q.C., who asked his clerk how many cases he was engaged in on the following day, and found that they were seven. So he said to his clerk: "I don't think that is really fair to the clients; you had better return one of them.")

It is odd that, when a conscientious barrister tells his clients in ample time that he really must return their case because he has little prospect of being free to give it proper attention, he is almost always met by entreaties to hold on to the case and attend as much as he can.

Returning to the progress of a case, let me show the stages through which the actual hearing will pass. The first step is that the plaintiff's Q.C. or, if the plaintiff has no Q.C., or if he is absent (he does his best to be present at the start), his junior, "opens the case", that is, he gives the judge a narrative account of the case from the plaintiff's point of view. This is one of the most important pieces of work in most cases, and a skilful and frank counsel can set a case on the way to victory by a good opening speech. He will very often indicate what the defendant —so far as he knows from the pleadings or elsewhere—will say about any particular incident. In cases where there is a lot of correspondence to be dealt with, as there often is, he will read not only the letters which help his client but those which are helpful to the judge's understanding of the case, as well as any that the defendant's counsel asks him to read. If the case involves any question of law, he will probably tell the judge briefly how the question arises, and will outline his contentions on them. (Fuller argument is generally better left until later, when it can be seen what exact facts have been proved.)

If the opening speech is made well, the judge will know at the end of it the salient facts of the case, the real issues, and the main contentions of both sides. Although cases very often take unexpected turns at one stage or another, he will also be able to feel that it is highly unlikely that some important fact that the plaintiff has not disclosed will turn up in the later stages of the case, and make him reshape his first impressions.

When a case is tried with a jury, which as I have already said is not very often, the opening speech will be addressed to the jury, whilst the judge of course will listen. The opening will not be basically different from what it would be if there were no jury, but it will be painted with a broader brush, and perhaps couched in somewhat simpler English and be delivered more slowly, for the benefit of the inexperienced laymen who form the jury. Counsel may be less frank in stating the difficulties of his own case or giving the defendant's case, for he will know that the opening of a case to a jury often shapes their attitude for good and all, so that they are not very willing to accept the defendant's version of a case about which the plaintiff's counsel has already told them.*

All that counsel can say to a jury about any question of law is that the judge will tell them the law, and they will take it from him, but that counsel suggests that what the judge may tell them is so and so.

The next stage in a case comes with the calling of the plaintiff's witnesses. They go into the witness-box one by one, take the oath, and give their evidence in answer to questions put to them by one or other of the plaintiff's counsel. Witnesses are of necessity called in almost every case (outside Chancery courts), for every fact on which a party relies, unless it is

* Addressing a jury is a highly-skilled matter, and I have had relatively little experience in it. One has little opportunity in any particular case to learn—apart from their verdict—what did or did not appeal to the jury in the way one dealt with them. But in one very long and interesting jury case, which I won, I did chance to get messages some time after from two of the jurymen, offering friendly criticism of the way I had conducted the case. The one said: "You are very good at your work, but you should remember that jurymen are rather simple; you should go slower, and say things several times, to give them a chance to grasp them." The other said: "You are very good at your work, but you should not assume that jurymen are as simple as you seem to think. You don't need to tell them things twice."

admitted—either in the pleadings, or by formal letter, or by statement of counsel at the hearing—must be proved, and proof can generally only come from clear statements in the correspondence or by the evidence of witnesses. There are often points on which the burden of proof is on the other side, so that if there is no evidence to "discharge" this burden the fact is taken as proved in favour of the plaintiff. Of course the defendant may seek to give evidence that will determine the point in his favour, and the plaintiff must deal with that possibility. In theory he should wait to see if the defendant calls such evidence, and then seek himself to call "rebutting" evidence; but in practice, for convenience, the plaintiff will call his evidence on such a point along with the rest of his evidence.

The only other manner in which evidence may be dispensed with is on matters which are said to be "of judicial notice", i.e., to be taken as known to the court without proof, such as the days of the week and the geographical situation of places and countries. (In certain cases, such as the existence of a state of war between various countries, and the recognition of a foreign state, the judge must ask the Foreign Office, and accept its answer as conclusive, even when he knows that the answer is dishonest, untrue, or incomprehensible.) "Judicial notice" goes pretty wide, but it is probably narrower in Britain than in most countries. For example, it was thought necessary in Scotland to have an express decision of the courts that notice could be taken of the fact that whisky is intoxicating.*

How must counsel for the plaintiff (and the same thing stands for the defendant when his turn comes) conduct himself when he comes to call his witnesses? To begin with, he must not ask leading questions, except on matters that are not in dispute, such as names, addresses, occupation, and such matters.†

* For the opposite extreme, I could quote a criminal case in West Germany in 1959–60, in which my clients, the accused, sought to prove as part of their defence that the foreign policy of the West German Republic was likely to lead to war. The court ruled that they could not be heard to argue this, since it was bound to "take judicial notice" that Chancellor Adenauer was a man of peace!

† Many laymen—and, I think, most detective writers—do not understand what a leading question is. It is not one which is awkward or difficult to answer, but is simply one which suggests to the witness what his answer should be: For example, "Did he then kick you on the shin?" is a leading question, and the proper question should be: "What did he then do?" The common sense of the rule is obvious, for many witnesses are called in the hope that they will say something more favourable to the side calling them than their memory justifies, and leading questions are very encouraging in that direction.

Even apart from that restriction, the task of counsel calling a witness is not too simple, for he must be ready to meet objections raised by the other side to any question he may put, on the ground that it, or rather the answer it is designed to elicit, is irrelevant or inadmissible. (It will be irrelevant if it is not material to any issue raised by the pleadings, i.e., if it does not help to prove or disprove any relevant fact, and it will be inadmissible if the way in which it is intended to prove some fact, even relevant, is not permissible under the law of evidence, e.g., if it be hearsay. Objections are often raised. They may annoy the judge, and are almost certain to annoy a jury, who suspect at once that the objector is trying to exclude something which they would like to hear, and which would injure the objector's case. So counsel do not like to object unnecessarily, but they are in the dilemma that, as they do not know what the answer would be, and thus do not know how much it would harm the case which it is their duty to conduct in the interests of their client, they are bound to assume that the other side is asking the question because it thinks it will help it, and that they ought therefore to exclude it if they can.)

The plaintiff himself will probably be among the witnesses, for normally he can testify to something relevant. It is usual, although there is no rule about it, that he should be called as the first witness. There are of course cases, sometimes amusing ones, in which the plaintiff is a man of bad character or reputation, who fears that, if he is called, he will have to admit in cross-examination to a long string of rascalities, and perhaps to serious crimes, in his record, and is therefore anxious to make out his case without giving evidence himself. This situation arises most commonly in actions for libel or slander. The plaintiff can often prove the publication of the libel or slander without himself testifying, for the publication has to be a third party to make it actionable, and those third parties can prove it. A rascally plaintiff rightly fears that if cross-examination damaged him in the eyes of the jury the latter might return a verdict for the defendant, or one for him with small or even with contemptuous damages (i.e., a farthing when that coin was current, and today a penny). The defendant's counsel can always comment strongly on the fact that "the plaintiff dare not give evidence", but he cannot tell the jury what the plaintiff would have had to admit in cross-examination if he had done so. This is all linked with another peculiarity of the system, namely that "bad character" of this sort cannot be proved by evidence by the other side as part of their case, because it is not strictly relevant to any issue in the case, but that nevertheless anyone who gives evidence can be asked in cross-examination not only questions relevant to the issues but also those relevant only to "credit" (another lawyers' word, meaning in reality credibility, or character), on the ground that they may help to show that the evidence of the witness is less likely to be reliable than it would be if he had a good character. (But the answers of a witness to questions "to credit" must be accepted in the sense that evidence cannot be called to contradict what the witness has said, except in the event of the witness denying that he has been convicted of criminal offences.)* I will deal with cross-examination to character a little later.

The next stage (if I may call it so) in the hearing comes in bits, as often as the plaintiff calls witnesses. It consists in the cross-examination of the plaintiff's witnesses by the defendant, as and when the evidence they give for the plaintiff—called "evidence in chief"—comes to an end. This is the first stage at which the defendant has any opportunity to take any but a silent part in the case (apart from the opportunity he may have had to raise objections to the admissibility of any questions to the witnesses). Technically, the cross-examiner's right is limited to asking questions, but he will often use his questions as a means of giving some indication of what his answer to the plaintiff's case is, especially when he is cross-examining the plaintiff or anyone else who has played a prominent part in the matters constituting the subject of the action.

Cross-examination is often a highlight of a hearing, and may at times determine the result of the case, either in favour of the cross-examining side or against it. It looks easy enough to the outsider, but is in fact a difficult and delicate operation, in

---

* I should add it is not practicable for the defendant to call the plaintiff as a witness, in order to get him into the witness-box somehow. It is legally permissible, but the litigant who calls a witness cannot cross-examine him, and is said to "put the witness forward as a witness of truth" and to be bound by what he says. This does not mean that he cannot call other witnesses to say the opposite, but it does mean that the litigant is making what the witness says "part of his own case".

which one unnecessary or careless question may open up for the benefit of the other side many avenues of evidence that would otherwise not be open to it—as I will explain in a moment—or may harm the cross-examiner's case in other ways. All the complications of this matter are one more illustration of the technicality of the work of litigation and of the way in which the employment of skilled and costly advocates may help the longer purse.

In some respects the cross-examiner, although his task is more difficult than that of the examiner in chief, has a freer hand. For example, he may ask leading questions, for the witness, belonging so to speak to the other side, is not likely to be "led" to say something to help the "leader". He does not have to justify every question he asks by showing that it is relevant to the issues, for it is enough that it is relevant to the "credit" of the witness. Looking at cross-examination as a whole, one sees that there are in substance three main fields for it.

Firstly, in many cases, one may need to get from the witness some evidence which helps one's own case. This is often useful when, as it may happen, the witness is better informed on the point than one's own witness, or one's own possible witness might make a bad impression or make unwanted admissions in cross-examination and so should not be called if it can be avoided.

Secondly, the cross-examiner not only may but must put to the witness the version which his witnesses are expected to give on any point to which the witness has spoken in "chief", so as to give him an opportunity of admitting, denying, or explaining. (Failure to do this may in some cases lead to the defendant not being allowed to get his witnesses to speak on the matter when his turn comes, and will always lead to the suspicion, indeed the accusation, that the defendant's version had not been put to the plaintiff's witnesses at the proper time because it had not then been concocted.)

Thirdly, the defendant's counsel may put to any witness questions "to credit", a phrase which I have already explained. Of course, much of the cross-examination on mattters relevant to the issues may already have gone some way to showing that the witness's evidence should not be accepted, because, for

H

example, it is inherently improbable, or contradicted by other witnesses or the documents.*

I must write something more about cross-examination to credit, as it is extremely important. As I have hinted, it can range very wide, for the conduct of the witness at any time and in any context may well be relevant to the question whether he is to be accepted as speaking the truth and—unless the witness is one whose honesty is accepted or is not even involved, since his evidence may be on some formal matter—it is difficult to rule out any question to credit (but that does not mean that it is wise or reasonable to roam over wide fields in the effort to discredit a witness). Cross-examination to credit has very often persuaded a judge or a jury not to accept the evidence of a witness—perhaps a vital one—who, before he was cross-examined, was almost certain to be accepted. But it has its dangers. To start with, if the witness denies what is suggested against him, it will often be taken by the judge or jury, since no evidence can in general be called to rebut the denial, that the defendant is just "throwing mud". This danger is well illustrated by the case I described earlier, in which the then Mr. F. E. Smith was engaged. And I had a curious case illustrating the same danger many years ago, which came from New South Wales to the Privy Council. The plaintiff, who ultimately became my client, was a man who had done many discreditable things in the past, but had recovered himself and built a good reputation. He was savagely libelled by a Sydney newspaper on charges of alleged misconduct of which he was in fact innocent, and he sued the paper for libel. His counsel opened the case, and put the plaintiff into the witness-box. The defendant's counsel then cross-examined him to credit for a week, on all his past rascalities, but asked him nothing about the libel itself. The plaintiff answered the questions as best he could, but of course had to admit a good deal. When his evidence was over, and his counsel "closed his case", i.e., said that he had no more evidence and that it was now the defendant's

---

* A minor difficulty of cross-examination on this sort of contradictory material is that it sometimes leads to argument between counsel and witness, which—even when couched in the form of question and answer—is not proper, and is indeed a waste of time. One lovable judge before whom I appeared in my early days would often say: "Don't try to convince the witness, Mr. Pritt; you never will. It is myself that you have to convince."

turn, the defendant's counsel announced that he would call no evidence. The position of the case in law was then that, the defendant having called no evidence to support his case, the plaintiff was entitled to a verdict from the jury for damages, which the jury could no doubt assess at a low figure if they thought right. But the old-fashioned procedure in New South Wales gave the plaintiff's counsel no right to address the jury at that stage, since the defendant had called no evidence. The judge failed to make the position clear to them. So the jury, thoroughly captured by the long cross-examination to credit, took the bit between their teeth and returned a verdict for the defendant. My client carried the matter to appeal in New South Wales, without success, and then to the Privy Council, where we put the matter right and obtained an order for a new trial, which the plaintiff duly won. The newspaper thus had to pay not only damages but the costs of both sides in two trials and two appeals.

There is still to be considered one of the major dangers of cross-examination, which I have already briefly mentioned, that the cross-examination (whether on relevant matters or "to credit", although it arises mostly in the latter case) may "open up" for evidence in re-examination (the stage in the examination of witnesses which comes after cross-examination, and is designed to give the plaintiff's counsel the opportunity to ask any questions necessary to clear up something that has been said in cross-examination). There is a common-sense rule that, if anything is raised in cross-examination, the plaintiff must be allowed to get in re-examination any evidence necessary to clear it up. If it be said or thought that this is going rather far afield, the answer always is that the defendant thought it worth while raising in cross-examination and can therefore hardly be heard to say that it is not worth while taking up in re-examination. In this way, many things which the plaintiff would greatly like to make public, but which he cannot develop himself as they are not strictly relevant to the issues, are brought out and made possible—possible, moreover, with all the advantages to the plaintiff that he may get them stated in re-examination—but the defendant still has no right to call evidence about them.

I have seen many cases in which, in this way, one careless

question may give the other side a great and otherwise un-obtainable advantage. An extreme illustration of this arose in one of the cases in Kenya involving Jomo Kenyatta, of which I shall write something in a later volume. The most important witness for the prosecution in the main case against Kenyatta and five of his colleagues had been bribed by the government with as much as £2,500 "in meal or in malt" to give evidence which Kenyatta, and I as his counsel, asserted was wholly false. The witness subsequently stated on oath in an affidavit that the whole of the evidence he had given against Kenyatta was false, and the government then prosecuted him for perjury; but instead of prosecuting him for perjury in the case against Kenyatta they charged him for perjury in saying in his affidavit that his original evidence was false! On his trial, therefore, the only question in substance was whether the story he had told about Kenyatta taking part in certain activities of the banned organisation "Mau Mau" was true or false, and on that Kenyatta gave evidence, being examined in the ordinary way by myself, and then cross-examined by the prosecution counsel. This cross-examination was in the main uneventful, but in one careless question the prosecutor did a bigger job by way of "opening up" than any other I can remember. He asked Kenyatta whether he could not have secured better treatment for his hundreds of thousands of supporters in the fight for colonial liberation if he had relied on the colonial government to recognise and remedy their grievances. At the time, the fight for liberation had not been won, the colonial government was still in power and outwardly secure, and Kenyatta was still in prison. This question "opened up" the whole immense field of the struggle for colonial liberation which at that moment, in the middle fifties, was near to a long series of victories, and thus gave Kenyatta an opportunity to state in re-examination the whole of his case for his previous work in Kenya, and indeed the whole case for the colonial liberation struggle. It may be that I ought to have sat silent and waited for re-examination, and then to have occupied three weeks or so in a small court house in a village 300 miles from Nairobi with questions to Kenyatta, in answer to each of which he could have delivered a lecture on one aspect or another of the liberation struggle, or on the many instances of bad faith, stupidity, or oppression by the colonial government. But, rightly or wrongly, I was merciful enough to say to the magistrate: "Technically, I have no right to object to this question, and I do not do so. Indeed, I welcome it. But I point out to the prosecution that, if it is asked, I shall re-examine the witness for at least three weeks on the results which would have followed if he had done as the prosecution suggests he should have done, and on the conduct of the colonial government which would lead him to say that these results would have followed."

The question was withdrawn.

The rules as to examining and cross-examining witnesses apply equally in criminal cases, but are rather more strictly observed there by prosecutors, who in non-political cases generally behave fairly to the accused, who until recently were often undefended and were often of limited intelligence. Any carelessness, and especially leading questions, might bring out evidence of things that did not really happen, or inadmissible evidence, leading to prejudice in the minds of the jury against which the conventional warnings by the judge to the jury to disregard such evidence are ineffective. In reference, however, to the cross-examination of the accused, the rules are very different, for historical reasons. Until the start of this century, accused were not allowed to give evidence at all, on the ground that they would be subject to great temptation to commit perjury, and would thus—since perjury was originally an ecclesiastical offence—add a burden on their souls to the burden on their body applied by the criminal courts. When at the beginning of this century the law was altered to permit the accused to give evidence if he wanted to do so, rather elaborate protection was given to him in relation to cross-examination. He may be cross-examined freely about the crime with which he is charged, but not to credit, and in particular not as to previous convictions (unless he has given evidence of his own good character or attacked the character of witnesses for the prosecution).

Looked at as a whole, cross-examination is a very valuable weapon for getting at the truth of a case. It is true that at times honest witnesses, unaccustomed to courts, may be bullied into looking untruthful when they are not, but this rarely happens, as judges are alert to protect them. And in many cases those who *are* seeking to tell a false story are well exposed by cross-examination. The system is used very fully not only in Britain but in all countries where "Anglo-Saxon" law prevails. It is little used in other systems. In pre-war Germany and in West Germany today, for example, whilst the rules of procedure would permit of its use in much the same way as in Britain, little is made of it. I took part in a long criminal case in West Germany in 1959–60, in which most of the prosecution witnesses were spies, informers, or other persons of bad character, but there was very little cross-examination either on the facts or to credit, and my German fellow-defenders told me that this was usual. As far as I could judge they might well have cross-examined on our lines, but they did not do so. (Their procedure does, however, provide other methods of impugning the reliability of a witness.)

It is an oddity of legal history that the finest example of shrewd and effective cross-examination on the best English lines is to be found in pre-war Germany, in a cross-examination by a defendant who was a layman and neither English nor German. He was the famous Bulgarian revolutionary patriot, Georgi Dimitrov, defending himself in 1933, at Leipzig, in the famous Reichstag Fire Trial. There, quite briefly, and with the rarest of all cross-examiners' virtues, namely, not a single unnecessary question, he reduced the powerful and arrogant Goering to gibbering rage, completely demolished his evidence, exposed him to the world for what he was, and left the Nazis with no option but to abandon all further ideas of staging "show trials".

So much for cross-examination and all its facets. Let me come back to the procedure in an ordinary case. After re-examination, a witness has finished, and is followed by the next. When all the witnesses have been called, the plaintiff "closes his case". It is then the turn of the defendant. His counsel opens his case with a speech, and then calls his witnesses, who are examined, cross-examined, and re-examined. Then the counsel for the two parties make their final speeches, in an order determined by rather elaborate rules. And the judge gives his judgment either then or later, or, as the case may be, the jury gives its verdict, and the judge gives judgment in accordance therewith.

Then comes, quite possibly, the question of appeal by the

unsuccessful party. In general, every verdict, judgment, or other decision of the High Court of Justice can be carried to appeal before the Court of Appeal (and, if leave be given, from there to the House of Lords), and there re-argued both on questions of law and questions of fact (on the latter, naturally, the Court of Appeal pays a good deal of attention to the fact that the trial judge had the advantage of seeing the witnesses give evidence, and forming his estimate of their honesty).

Save in rare cases, evidence is not called on appeals, which are argued on the footing of the written or printed record of the proceedings. A substantial number of appeals are brought every year, and nearly half of them are "allowed", i.e., the decision at first instance is held to be wrong. Generally, but not necessarily, the same counsel argue the appeal as appeared at first instance, but it is not uncommon for one or both sides to bring in an additional Q.C. who is thought to be especially skilled in appellate work, which is generally held to be more difficult (but to my mind, at any rate for counsel who know their law well, is much easier). Occasionally, of course, a disappointed client will change his whole "team", including even the solicitors, and I took part in one or two interesting cases where that was done with favourable results, winning cases in the House of Lords which had been lost in both the High Court and the Court of Appeal.

A system of appeals is obviously a necessity, not just in Britain but in all countries, but it is of course an additional source of expense, and thus of advantage to the long purse (although not quite as expensive as the proceedings at first instance, as there is less preparatory work and no witnesses).

I come now to the County courts, civil courts of substantial but limited jurisdiction. As I have said already, they sit in many towns, and thus provide litigants with justice at no great distance from their homes. They were originally designed expressly to be "poor men's courts", and most poor men's litigation goes to them, but a good deal of more substantial matters too. In terms of procedure, they are a simplified version of the High Court, but even with their simpler procedure the annual "County Court Practice", corresponding to the Supreme Practice which I described above, contains 2,800 pages and cites over 3,800 cases.

These courts can sit with juries, but do so even less frequently than does the High Court. There are no outstanding differences of procedure for me to discuss. Appeals go to the Court of Appeal, and with leave to the House of Lords, just as from the High Court of Justice. It was for a long time the rule—a typical example of giving the poor man poor justice—that appeals on questions of fact could not be carried from the County Courts, but that is no longer the case.

I turn now to criminal procedure, which shows a strong contrast to the elaborate civil procedure. I start with the pleadings in "major cases", i.e., trials at Assizes or Quarter Sessions after committal by magistrates. They start with an indictment, a short document specifying the crime or crimes charged, the day or days on which they are alleged to have been committed, and practically nothing else (but this scantiness of information is not in most cases a cause of injustice to the accused, since he will have heard or seen the whole of the prosecution evidence against him in the proceedings before the magistrates). There are a good many technical rules about these indictments, mostly helpful to the accused, with which I need not bother. But when it comes to the accused's turn to plead, the matter is as simple as it was centuries ago, when he was almost certainly illiterate. He does not plead at all until he comes up for his trial, and then he pleads by word of mouth (in almost all cases, with nothing more), and his plea is either "Guilty" or "Not Guilty".

The actual proceedings, the opening and final speeches, the witnesses, the summing-up, verdict, and sentence (or discharge), are similar to those in civil cases. Since a recent amendment of the law, the accused now has the right to the final speech in all cases.

As for appeals, the law started with a heavy prejudice against appeals by either side in criminal cases, but there is now a general right in convicted men in major cases to appeal, although leave is required on matters of pure fact. The appeals go to the Court of Appeal. Under quite exceptional circumstances, by leave, an appeal can go from the Court of Appeal to the House of Lords. The prosecution has normally no right of appeal, the jury's verdict of acquittal being regarded as virtually sancrosanct, but the prosecution may appeal from the Court of Appeal to the House of Lords under the same conditions as the accused. (The very limited right of the Court of Appeal to order a new trial has been stated above, in Chapter 9.)

The procedure in minor cases, before the magistrates, is extremely simple. The charge is made in informal language, and is read out to the accused, who pleads orally "Guilty" or "Not guilty". The one essential, as I mentioned at p. 66 of Book 1, is that it should be quite clear that a charge of some definite and specified offence, known to the law, is being made against the accused. Appeals go normally to the Quarter Sessions, and are there conducted by way of a re-hearing of the evidence. Questions of law can be taken by a rather cumbrous system to the High Court.

I can now come to the law of evidence, which plays a very important role in English procedure, although it is virtually unknown to "non-Anglo-Saxon" systems. These rules, substantially the same in civil and criminal proceedings, although more important and more strictly observed in the latter, are aimed at two objects. The first is that they should exclude evidence of anything not clearly relevant to some issue arising in the proceedings. That is after all sensible and businesslike, and presents no problem for this book. The second, much more important, is to prohibit any evidence being given that is not "the best evidence" to prove facts, whatever they be, that are relevant. "The best" is relatively easy to define. For example, if a document of any kind is in question, the original document must be produced, and a copy cannot be accepted unless there is very clear evidence as to why the original cannot be produced, and as to the accuracy of the copy. Such a rule is admirable as a counsel of perfection, but it may be carried too far, and there have to be exceptions. For example, many documents of a public nature are allowed by statute to be proved by various kinds of authenticated copies.

When one passes from documents to proof of facts, like the happening of any incident, or the making of any oral statement, the "best evidence" is that of some person who was personally present at the incident, or himself heard the statement made, and is not merely someone who relates it because someone else who did hear it has told him of it (this is called "hearsay").

The origins of the "best evidence" rule lie probably in two considerations. The first is the natural desire of any court to have before it the most reliable evidence of anything on which it has to base its decision, and the second is the particular and praiseworthy desire not to allow any evidence against any accused who, if found guilty of felony in the days when these rules were being built up would be sentenced to death, unless it was of the best available quality, and not just second-hand. Excellent as these rules are, they have been gradually developed, both in civil and criminal cases, to a point where they must seem both to jurors and to litigants to be designed to prevent much being said which they regard as helpful to the settlement of the conflict. On balance, there is much to be said in favour of the rules, especially if their rigours can be relaxed by reforms. But as they stand they tend to increase the expense and difficulty of litigation, with the results I have already mentioned. It would probably be better if we could gradually adopt a system under which these rules could be treated as what lawyers call matters of weight rather than admissibility, which means that when such second-class evidence is offered the courts should not simply say: "We cannot listen to that", but rather: "Well, we can consider that, but we shall not give it nearly as much weight as we would give to direct evidence." I have myself had some experience of litigation in jurisdictions where our rules of evidence do not apply, and have not found that questions of fact are dealt with with markedly less efficiency in the absence of such rules as ours. For the moment, the proper understanding and application of the rules remains one of the more important of the skills of advocates, and sometimes adds greatly to the cost of proving facts.

Finally, I must write a little about the interpretation of documents, whether they be just documents passing between the parties, such as letters, contracts, or deeds conveying property, or documents of more general importance, like Acts of Parliament or "delegated legislation". The courts should find it easy to deduce what people mean when they express themselves on paper, but it often proves to be more difficult and uncertain than might be expected. It is indeed notorious that divergent views among judges and lawyers on matters of interpretation are both greater and more uncertain than on most matters of law (I say matters of law, for the interpretation of documents is treated as a matter of law). I have given two typical illustrations of these difficulties in Chapter 4.

There are, of course, all sorts of rules as to how the court should make its interpretation. One begins, naturally, with a rule that it should look at the whole of the document, and at the intention with which it was drawn (that intention to be deduced only from what is to be found in the document itself, hence the importance which, as I said at p. 24 of Book 1, should be attributed to recitals in statutes). The next important rule is that the court should not take into account explanations as to what the parties meant to say, but only what they have actually said. For example, in construing an Act of Parliament, it must not even look at the debates in Parliament. It should of course have regard to the evil which a statute is designed to remedy, or the good it is intended to achieve, but even then it should elicit these from the statute itself.

I need not go into greater detail with the problem, and its innumerable sub-problems, but I must examine how far it has any political significance. Here one is concerned mainly with such matters as the interpretation and application of statutes such as those providing for compensation to workers for injuries sustained at work, which I discussed at length in Chapter 15 of Book 1, where there is a much greater scope for the element of class bias. Courts have often to interpret statutes to whose objects they are, perhaps unconsciously, hostile. By strict interpretation of what is called "remedial" legislation, it is possible to cut down severely the help that such legislation is designed to provide. As one progressive High Court judge said, very much off the record: "everyone knows that the judges sabotaged the Employers' Liability Act and the Workmen's Compensation Acts by their constructions of them, because they did not like the Acts".

Index